TEACH YOURSELF TO PLAY

GUITAR SONGS

T0081658

To access online content visit:
www.halleonard.com/mylibrary

Enter Code
6441-6363-1074-5846

ISBN 978-1-4950-4985-9

7777 W. Bluemound Rd. P.O. Box 13819 Milwaukee, WI 53213

Copyright © 2015 by HAL LEONARD CORPORATION
International Copyright Secured All Rights Reserved

For all works contained herein:
Unauthorized copying, arranging, adapting, recording, Internet posting, public performance,
or other distribution of the printed or recorded music in this publication is an infringement of copyright.
Infringers are liable under the law.

Visit Hal Leonard Online at
www.halleonard.com

CONTENTS

4 ANGIE *The Rolling Stones*

11 DAUGHTERS *John Mayer*

18 DRIVE *Incubus*

25 IRIS *Goo Goo Dolls*

35 LAYLA (UNPLUGGED) *Eric Clapton*

43 MR. JONES *Counting Crows*

53 MORE THAN WORDS *Extreme*

67 PATIENCE *Guns N' Roses*

79 WONDERWALL *Oasis*

89 YOU WERE MEANT FOR ME *Jewel*

95 Guitar Notation Legend

ANGIE
The Rolling Stones

Video Lesson – 12 minutes, 39 seconds

Standard Tuning: (low to high) E–A–D–G–B–E
Key of A minor

Guitar Tone:

- steel-string acoustic guitar

Chords:

Intro/Verse:

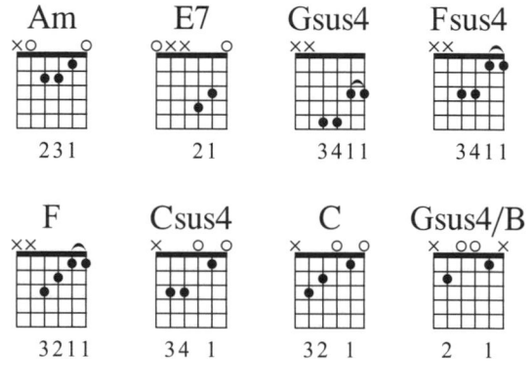

Chorus:

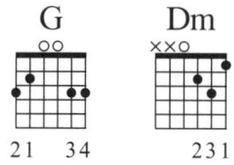

Techniques:

- Strum Variations: after you get the chords under your fingers, practice varying the strumming and picking on this tune. Change up the way you play the rhythms and arpeggios throughout so they are different than the notation. The Rolling Stones never play this chord structure the same way twice, and neither should you. There are endless variations possible and it's a great exercise in creativity and improvisation to generate as many as you can.
- Double Stops: fret the double stops by barring one finger across each fret. This will make the lick easier to grab as you move from chord strumming to fills and back.
- Harmonic: the very first note of the tune is a harmonic on the 12th fret of the A string. Lightly touch the string directly above the fret wire, without pushing down to the fretboard. Pluck the string and lift your finger off, allowing the harmonic to ring.

Angie

Words and Music by Mick Jagger and Keith Richards

© 1973 (Renewed 2001) EMI MUSIC PUBLISHING LTD.
All Rights for the U.S. and Canada Controlled and Administered by COLGEMS-EMI MUSIC INC.
All Rights Reserved International Copyright Secured Used by Permission

E7
Gsus4
G Fsus4 F
Cadd4
C
An - gie, where will it lead us from here? 1. With no
Chorus
G
Dm
Am
lov - in' in our souls and no mon - ey in our coats,
2., 3. See additional lyrics
C
F
G
uh, you can't say we're sat - is - fied.
To Coda
Am
E7
Gsus4
G Fsus4 F
An - gie, An - gie, you can't say we nev - er tried.

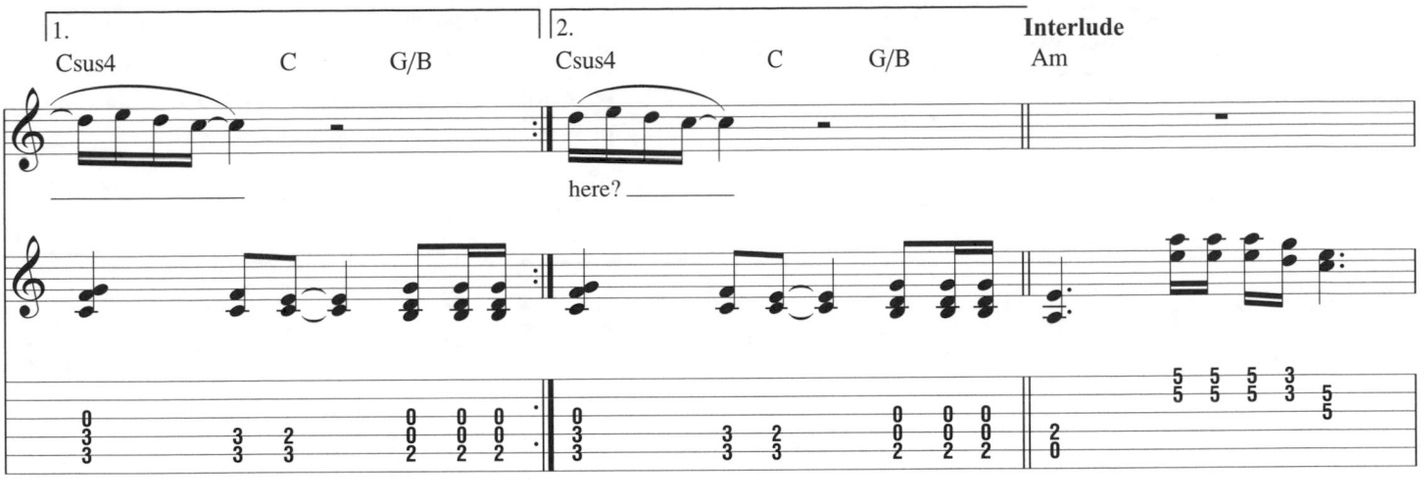
1.
Csus4 C G/B
2.
Csus4 C G/B
Interlude
Am
here?

E7 Gsus4 G Fsus4 F Csus4 C G/B Am

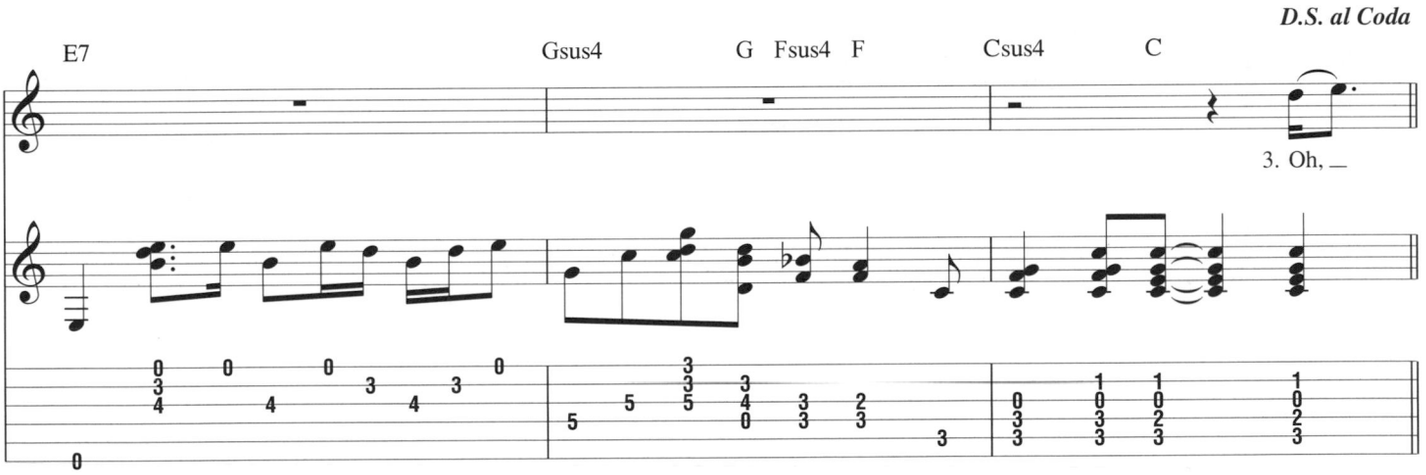
D.S. al Coda
E7 Gsus4 G Fsus4 F Csus4 C
3. Oh,

Coda
Interlude
Csus4 C G/B Am E7
bye? Yeah.
(An- gie, An - gie,

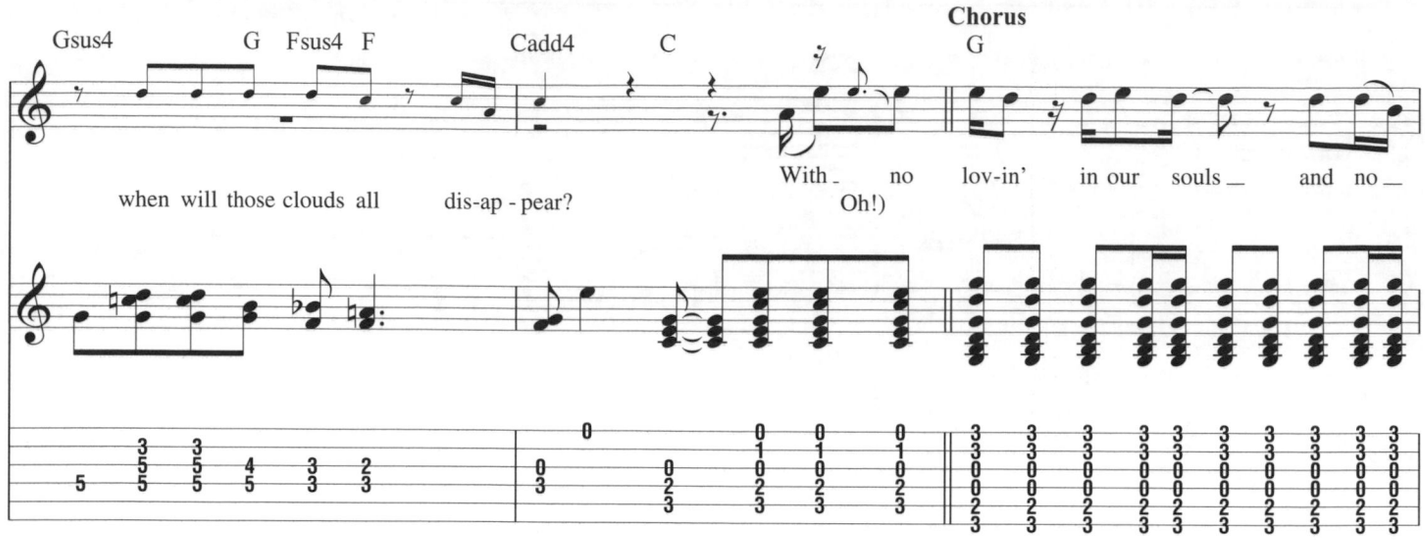
Chorus
Gsus4
G
Fsus4
F
Cadd4
C
G
when will those clouds all dis-ap - pear?
With no lov-in' in our souls and no
Oh!)

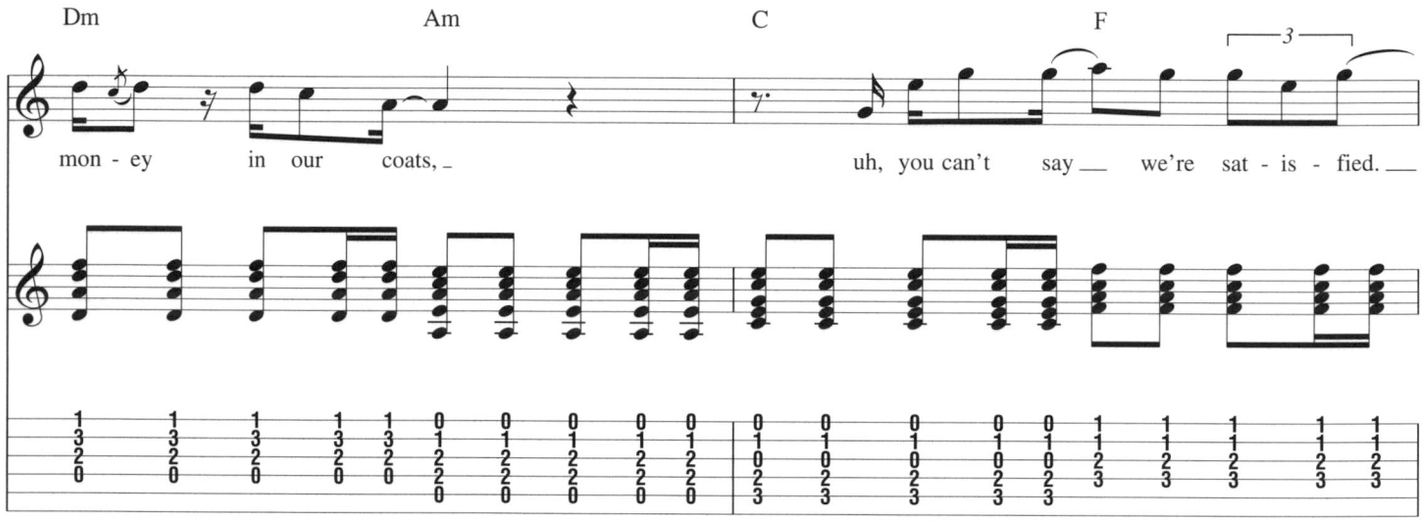
Dm
Am
C
F
3
mon - ey in our coats,
uh, you can't say we're sat - is - fied.

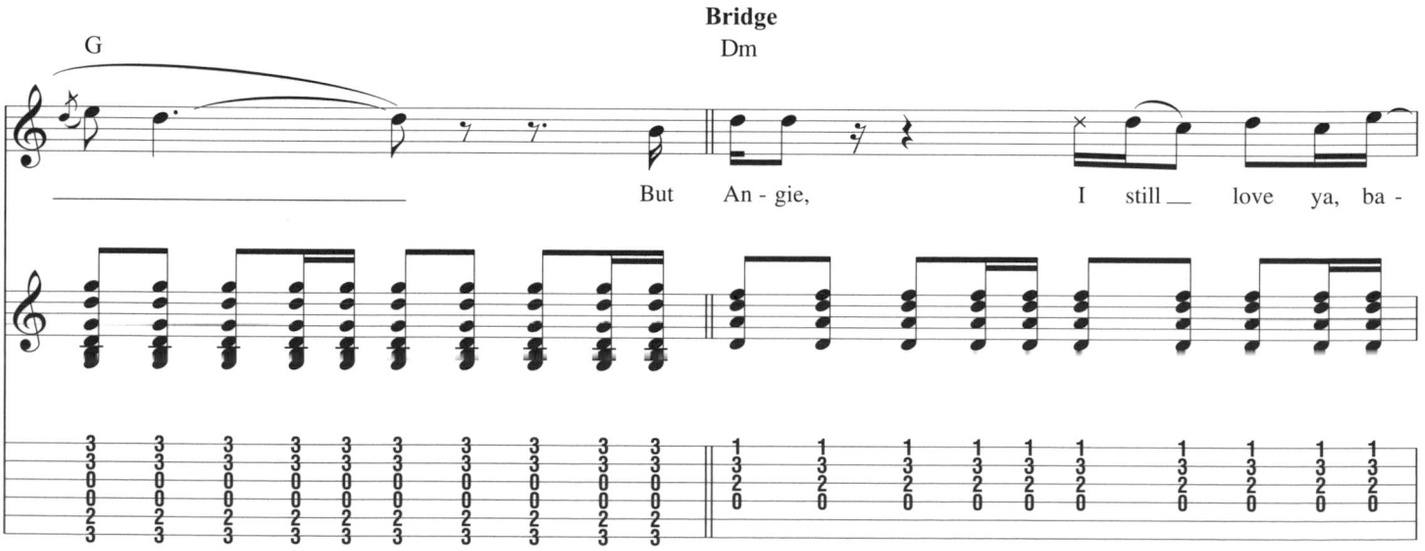
Bridge
G
Dm
But An - gie, I still love ya, ba -

Am
Dm
- by.
Ev - 'ry-where I look I see your eyes.

Am
Dm
Uh, there ain't a wom - an that comes

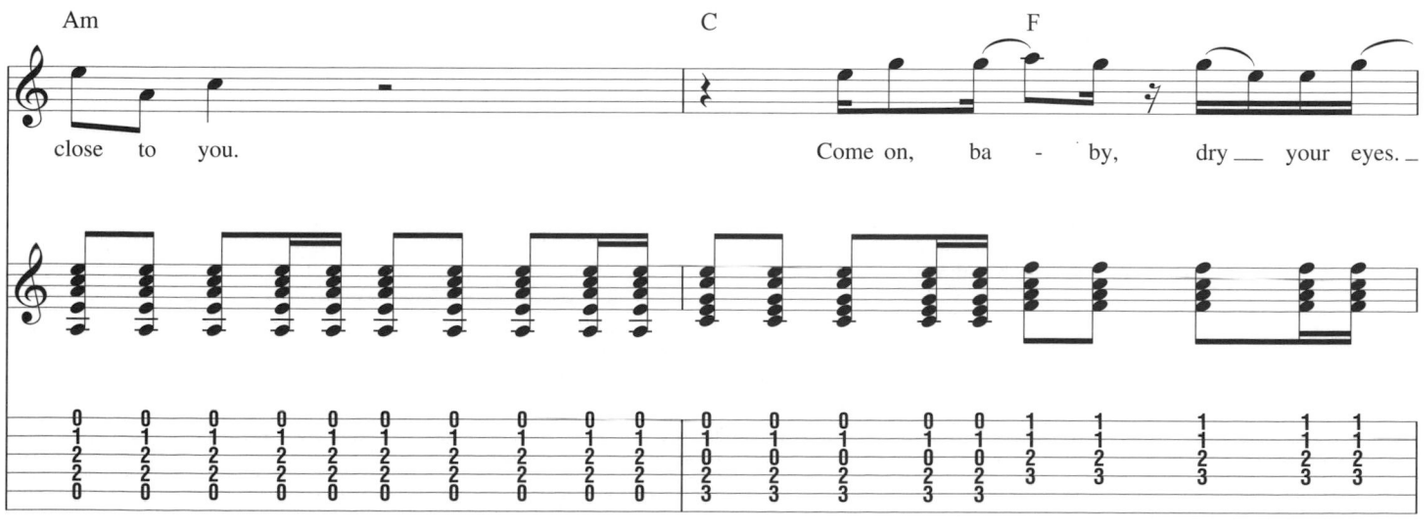
Am
C
F
close to you.
Come on, ba - by, dry your eyes.

Additional Lyrics

2. A-Angie, you're beautiful, yes,
But ain't it time we said goodbye?
A-Angie, I still love ya.
Remember all those nights we cried?

Chorus 2. All the dreams we held so close
Seemed to all go up in smoke.
Uh, let me whisper in your ear.
Whispered: Angie, Angie
Where will it lead us from here?

Chorus 3. Oh, Angie, don't you weep,
All your kisses still taste sweet.
I hate that sadness in your eyes.
But Angie, Angie,
A-ain't it time we said goodbye?

DAUGHTERS
John Mayer

Video Lesson – 21 minutes, 20 seconds

Standard Tuning: (low to high) E–A–D–G–B–E
Key of D

Guitar Tone:

- acoustic guitar or clean tone electric
- light reverb

Chords:

Verse 1:

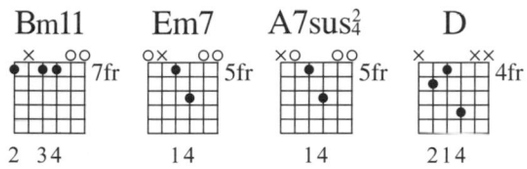

Chorus:

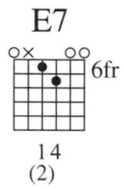

Verse 2:

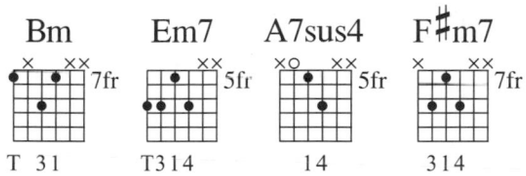

Bridge:

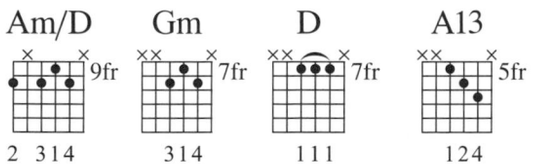

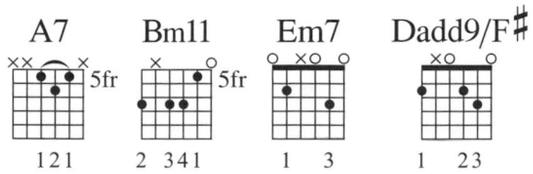

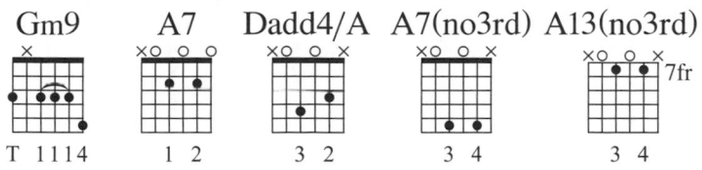

Scales/Arpeggios:

Intro/Interlude:

D Major Scale

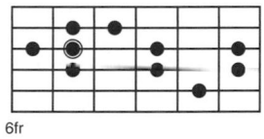

Techniques:

- Strumming: for the Verse and Chorus, strum the eighth note with a downstroke, and the sixteenth notes with alternating down-up-down-up strokes.
- Vibrato: shake the note up and down, creating a little series of quick bends and releases. Be sure to keep your wrist loose!
- Thumb-Fretting: some of the chords in the song involve fretting the 6th string with your thumb. This allows for more use of the other fingers. If this technique isn't comfortable for you, feel free to fret the chords with the other fret-hand fingers.
- String Bending: bending on an acoustic can be tough! Make sure you use support fingers behind the fretted note.
- Open-String Chords: be sure to stand your fret-hand fingers up straight for the arpeggiated chords in the last two measures of the Bridge. Make sure those open strings are ringing clearly and not getting muted by a flattened finger.

Daughters

Words and Music by John Mayer

Copyright © 2003 Specific Harm Music
All Rights Administered by Goodium Music, Inc., c/o Cal Financial Group, 700 Harris Street, Suite 201, Charlottesville, VA 22903
International Copyright Secured All Rights Reserved

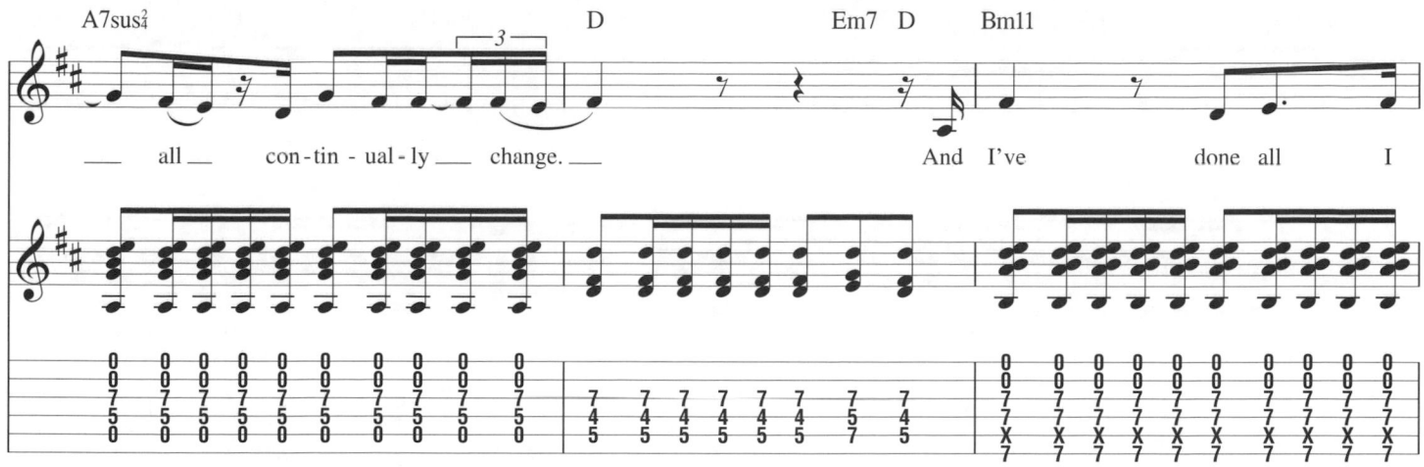
A7sus4
D
Em7 D
Bm11
all con-tin-ual-ly change.
And I've done all I

Em7
A7sus4
D
Em7
can to stand on her steps with my heart in my hand.
Now

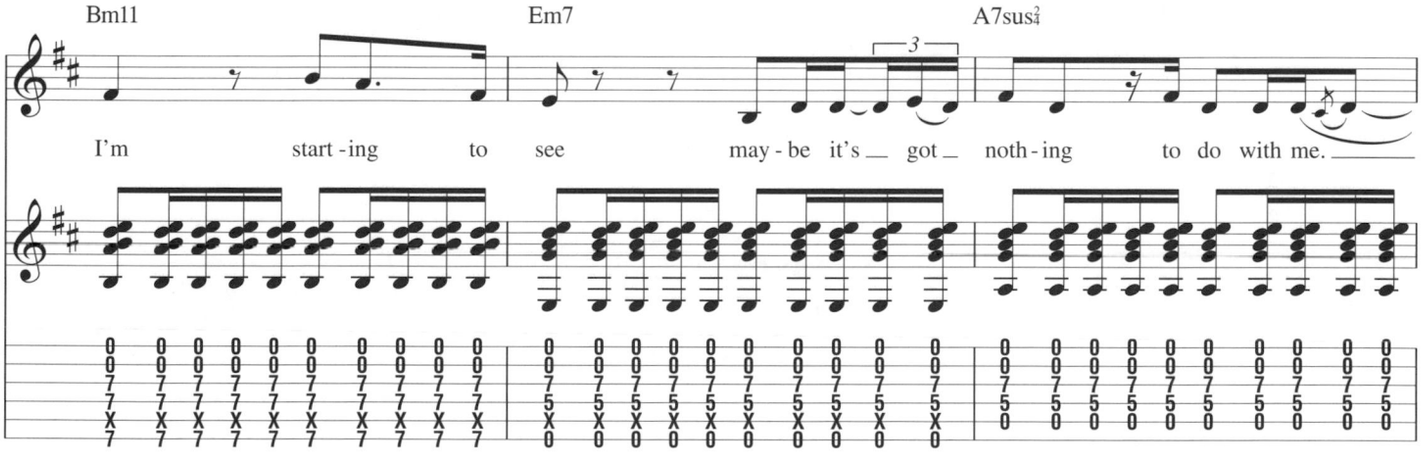
Bm11
Em7
A7sus4
I'm start-ing to see may-be it's got noth-ing to do with me.

Chorus
D
Bm11
E7
A7sus4
D
Fa-thers, be good to your daugh-ters.

To Coda 1

To Coda 2

Interlude

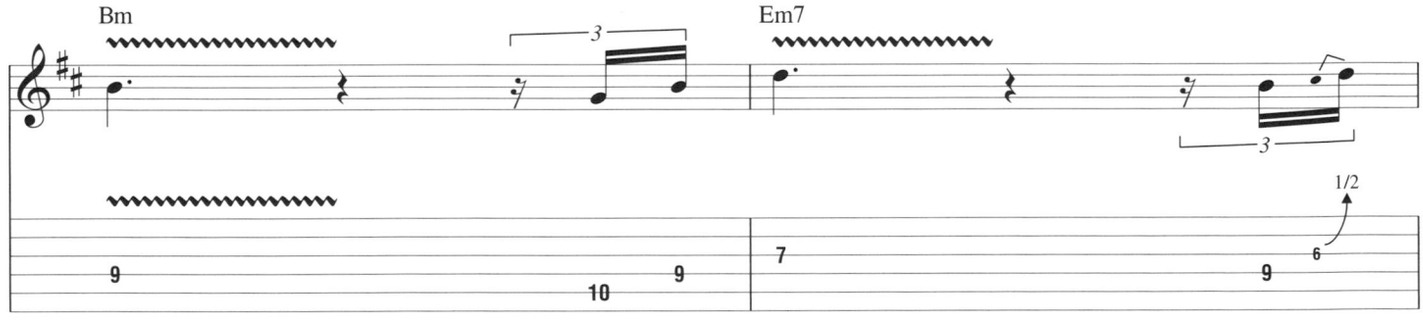

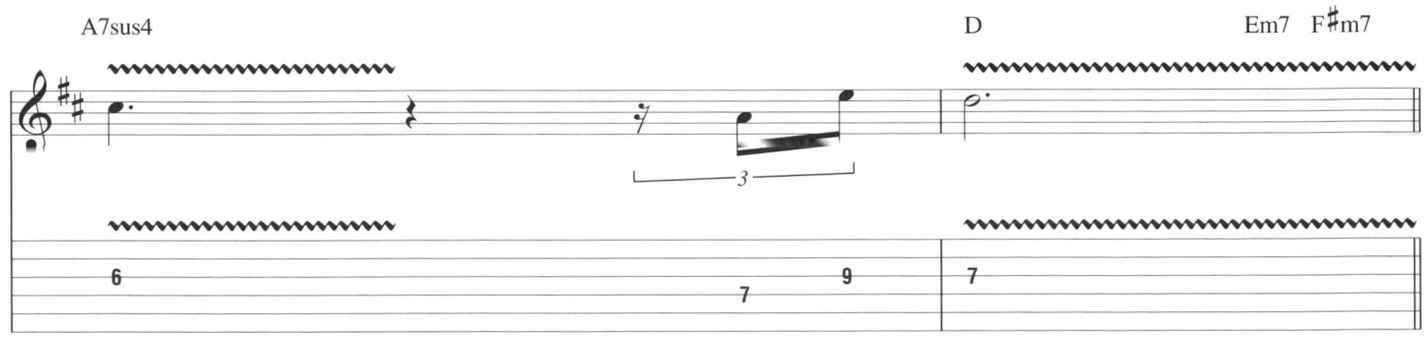

Verse
Bm
Em7
A7sus4
2. Oh, you see that skin? It's the same she's been stand - ing in
*T = Thumb on 6th string
D
Em7
F♯m7
Bm
Em7
since the day she saw him walk - ing a - way. Now she's
D.S. al Coda 1
A7sus4
D
Em7
F♯m7
left clean - ing up the mess he made. So

Coda 1

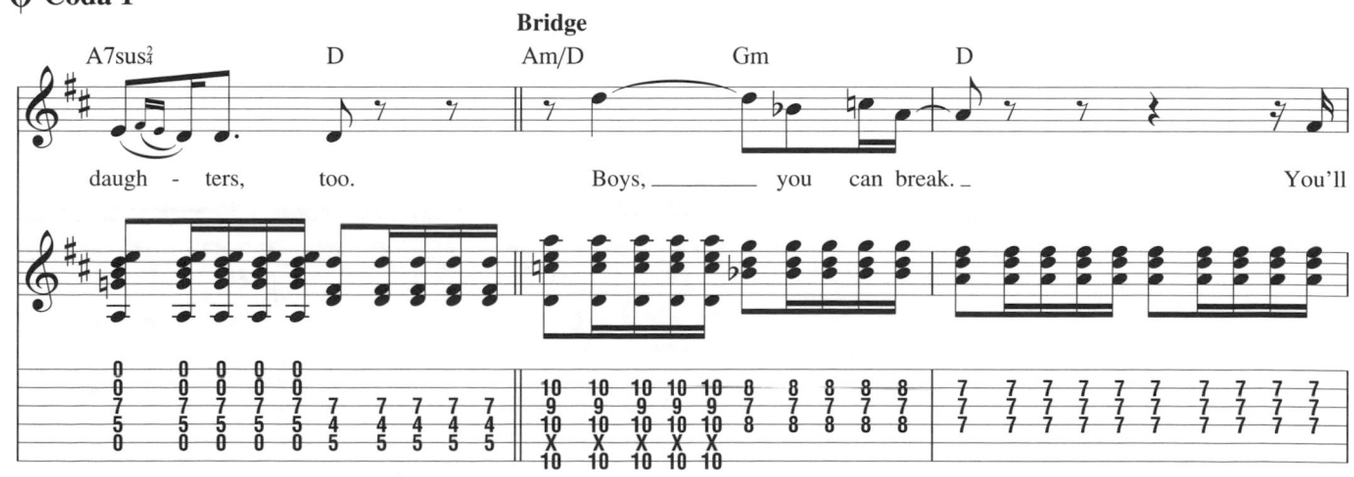
Bridge
A7sus4
D
Am/D
Gm
D
daugh - ters, too. Boys, you can break. You'll

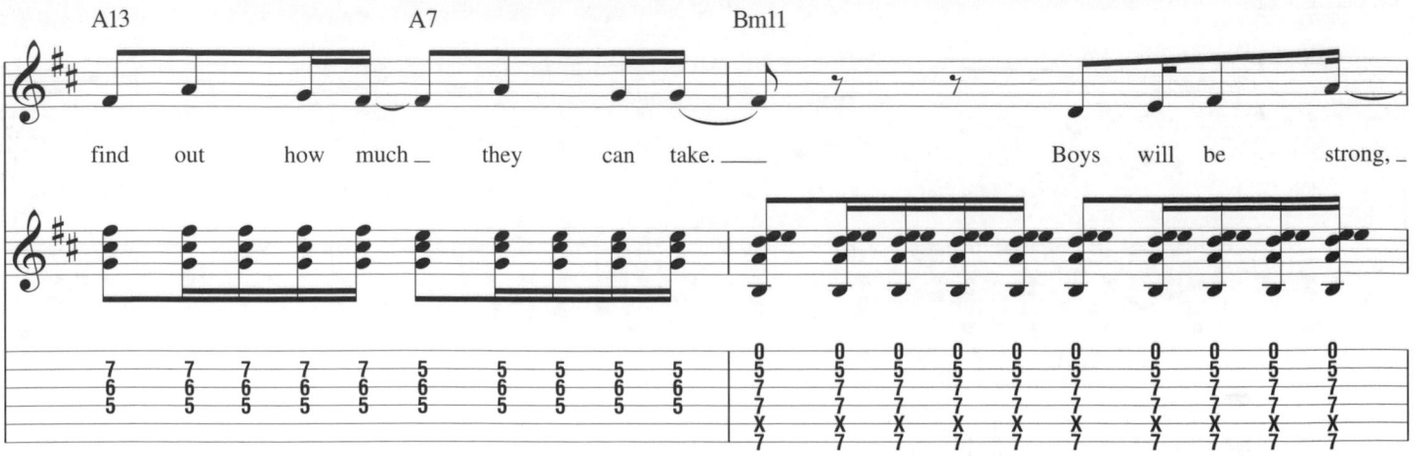
A13
A7
Bm11
find out how much they can take.
Boys will be strong,

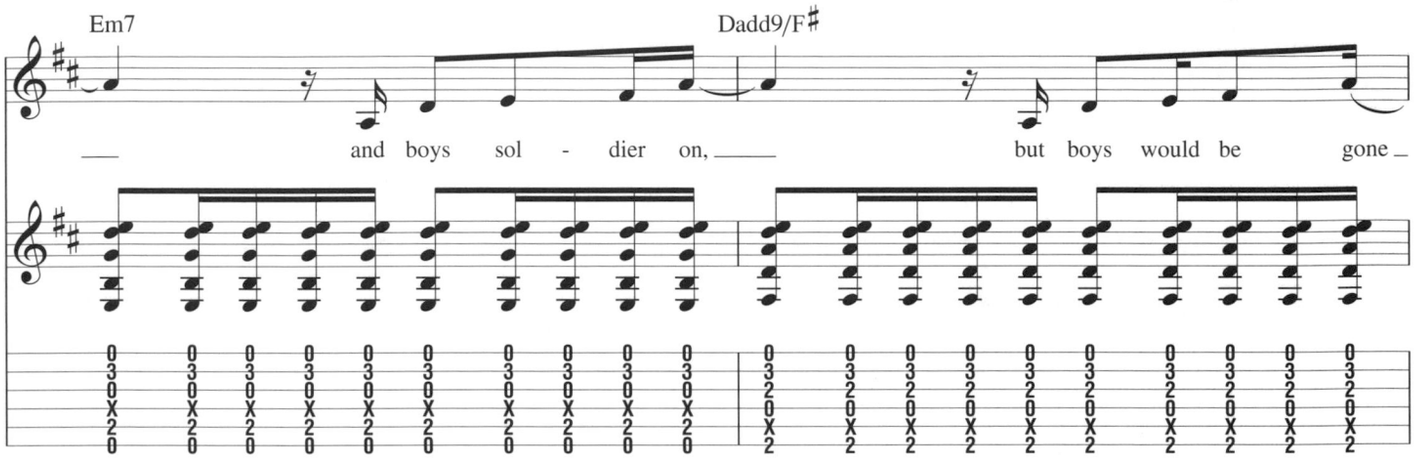
Em7
Dadd9/F♯
and boys sol - dier on,
but boys would be gone

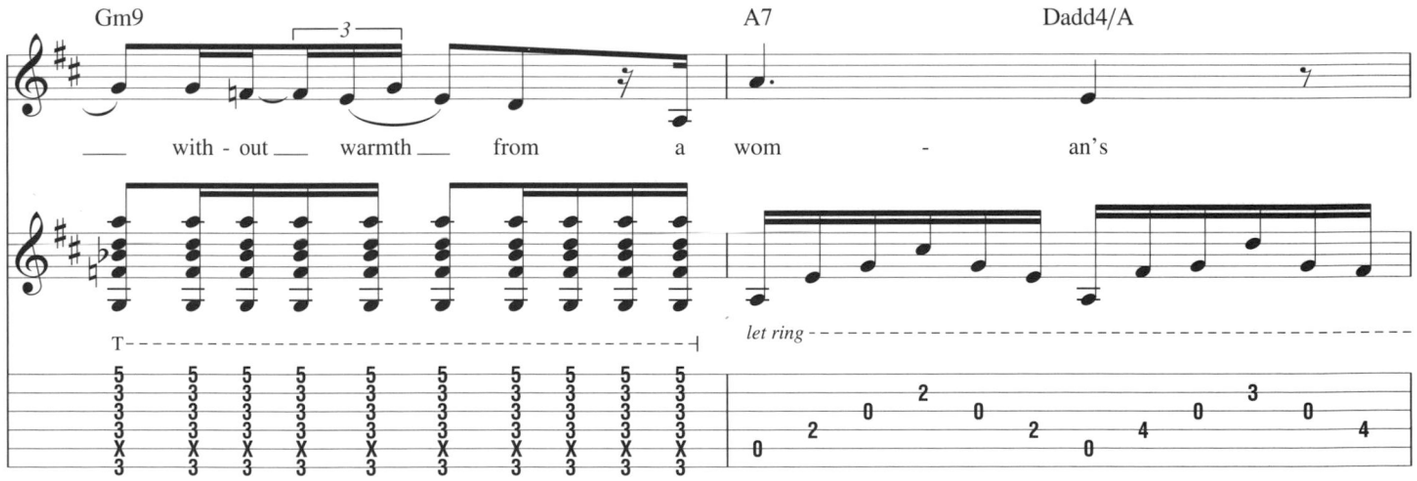
Gm9
A7
Dadd4/A
with - out warmth from a wom - an's
let ring

Interlude

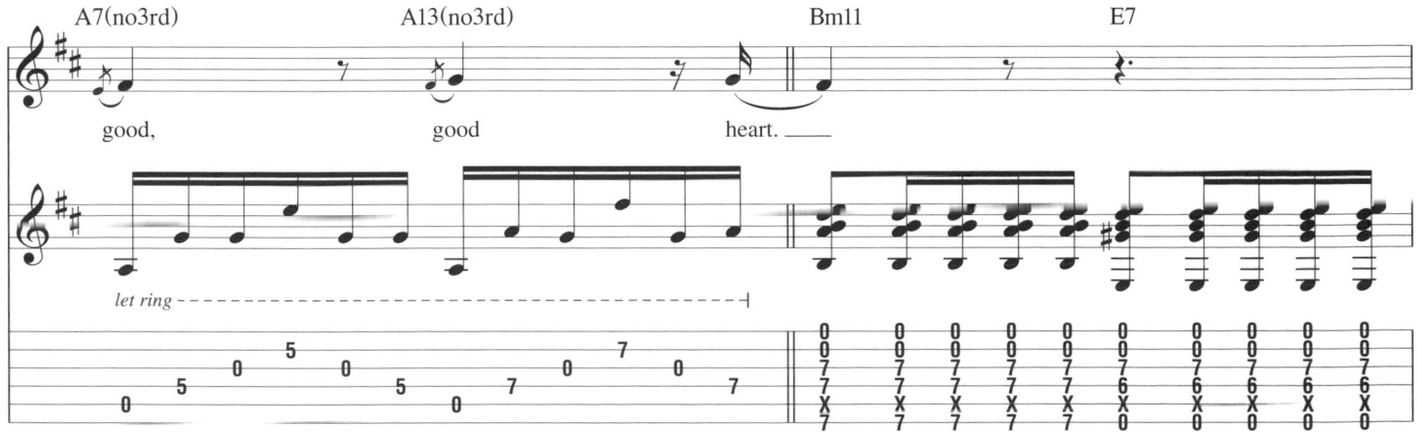
A7(no3rd)
A13(no3rd)
Bm11
E7
good,
good
heart.
let ring

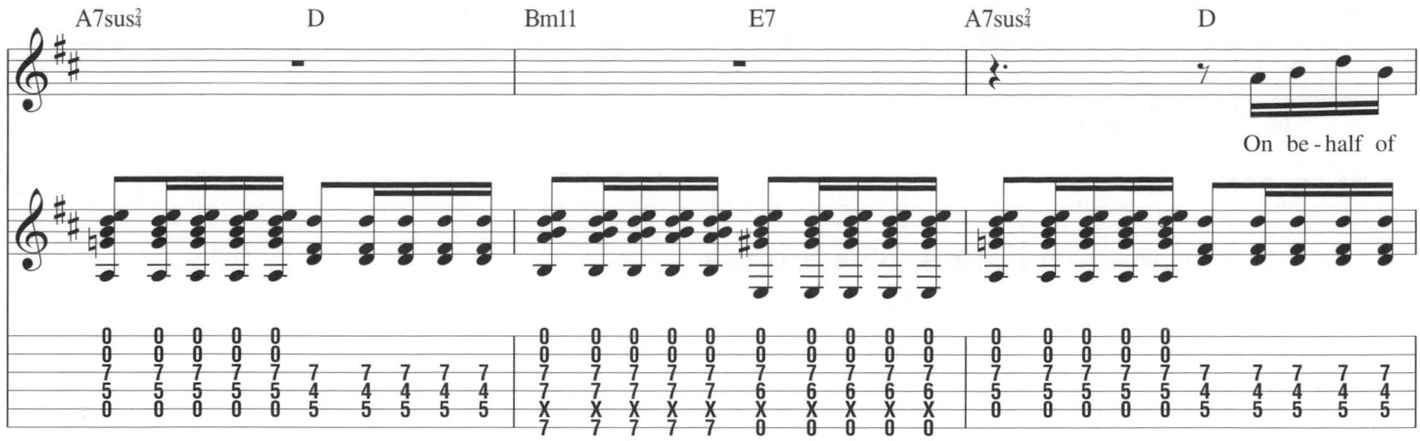
A7sus4 D Bm11 E7 A7sus4 D
On be-half of

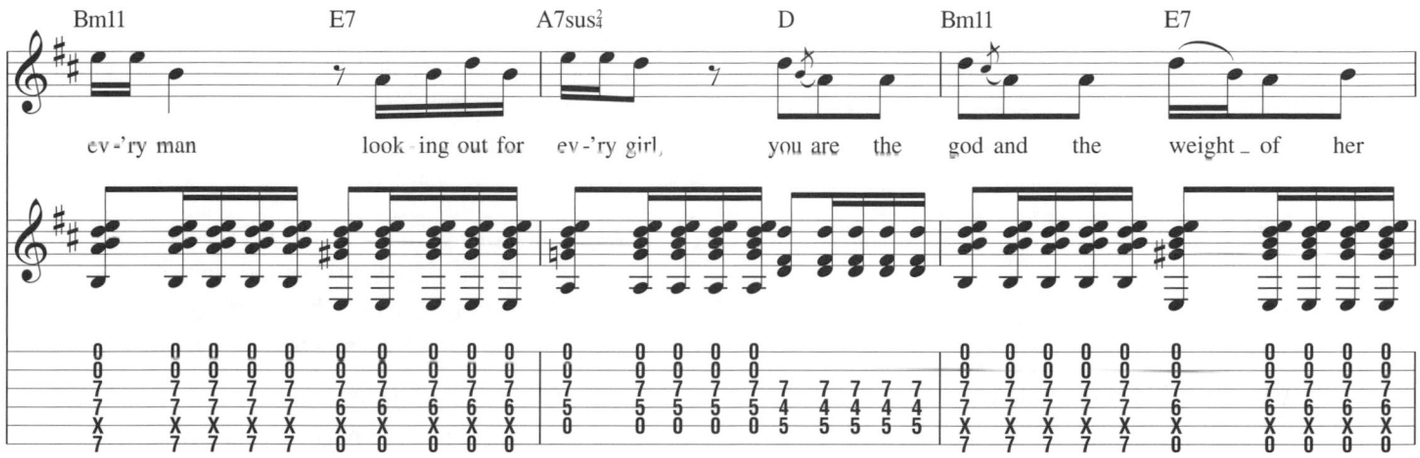
Bm11 E7 A7sus4 D Bm11 E7
ev-'ry man look ing out for ev-'ry girl, you are the god and the weight of her

D.S. al Coda 2
A7sus4 D
world. So

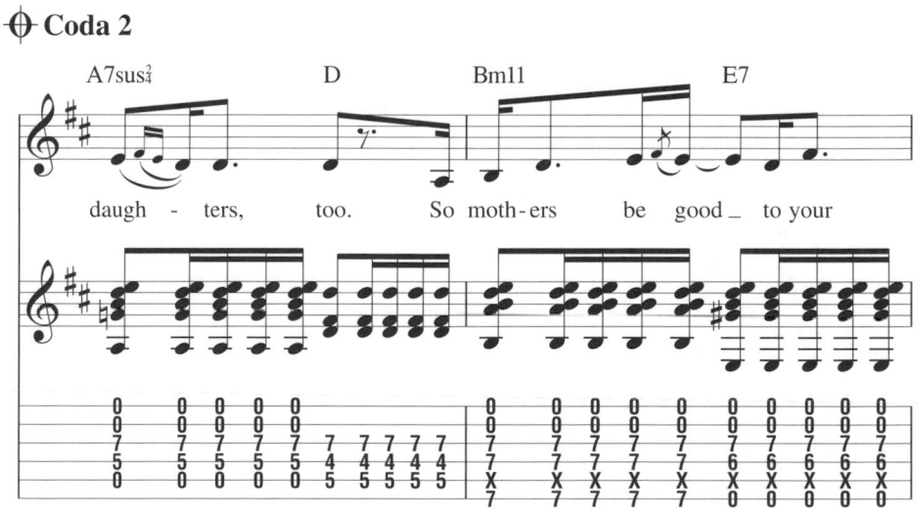
Coda 2
A7sus4 D Bm11 E7
daugh - ters, too. So moth-ers be good to your

A7sus4 D Bm11 E7 A7sus4 D
daugh - ters, too. So moth-ers be good to your daugh - ters, too.

DRIVE
Incubus

Video Lesson – 9 minutes, 35 seconds

Standard Tuning: (low to high) E–A–D–G–B–E
Key of E minor

Guitar Tone:

- Guitar Tone 1:
  - acoustic guitar or clean tone electric
  - light reverb
- Guitar Tone 2 (Interlude):
  - electric guitar
  - light distortion
  - light reverb
  - Leslie effect
  - bridge pickup
  - EQ: bass – 5, mid – 6, treble – 7

Chords:

Intro:

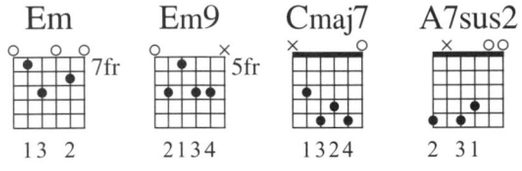

Pre-Chorus:

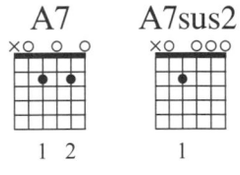

Techniques:

- Muted Strums: keep your fret hand lightly in contact with the strings, being careful not to accidentally fret any notes by pressing down too hard. Strum the muted strings, producing a "click" type sound. You can also assist the damping by using your pick hand to palm mute the strings near the bridge.
- Open-String Chords: most of the chords in this song involve a mixture of fretted notes and open strings. Make sure to fret these with the tips of your fret-hand fingers, allowing the open strings to ring clearly.
- Grace-Note Hammer-Ons/Slides: for the single-note solo in the Interlude, the small-sized grace notes don't have any rhythmic value, so move on to the attached second note as quickly as possible (whether it's a hammer-on or slide). Grace notes are also indicated with smaller numbers in the tab.
- Pick Slide: at the end of the last Pre-Chorus, you'll encounter a pick slide. Rub the edge of your pick down the strings, producing a scratchy sound. This will create ridges in the pick, so use an area of it that you don't typically employ for picking the strings.

Drive

Words and Music by Brandon Boyd, Michael Einziger, Alex Katunich, Jose Pasillas II and Chris Kilmore

Intro

Moderately slow ♩ = 90

Em Em9 Cmaj7 A7sus2

Play 4 times

mf

let chords ring throughout

Verse

Em Em9 Cmaj7 A7sus2

1. Some - times I feel the fear of un -
2. *See additional lyrics*

Em Em9 Cmaj7 A7sus2

cer - tain - ty sting - ing clear.

Em Em9 Cmaj7 A7sus2

And I, I can't help but ask my - self how much I'll

© 1999 EMI APRIL MUSIC INC. and HUNGLIKEYORA MUSIC
All Rights Controlled and Administered by EMI APRIL MUSIC INC.
All Rights Reserved International Copyright Secured Used by Permission

Em
Em9
Cmaj7
A7sus2
let the fear take the wheel and steer.
Pre-Chorus
Cmaj7
A7
A7sus2
A7
A7sus2
It's driv - en me be - fore, and it seems to have a vague,
See additional lyrics
Cmaj7
A7
A7sus2
A7
A7sus2
haunt - ing mass ap - peal.
Cmaj7
A7
A7sus2
A7
A7sus2
But late - ly I'm be - gin - ning to find that I

Cmaj7
A7
should be the one be - hind the wheel.
Chorus
Em
Em9
Cmaj7
A7sus2
Em
Em9
What - ev - er to - mor - row brings, I'll be there with o - pen arms
Cmaj7
A7sus2
Em
Em9
and o - pen eyes, yeah. What - ev - er to - mor -
To Coda
Cmaj7
A7sus2
Em
Em9
3
- row brings, I'll be there, I'll be

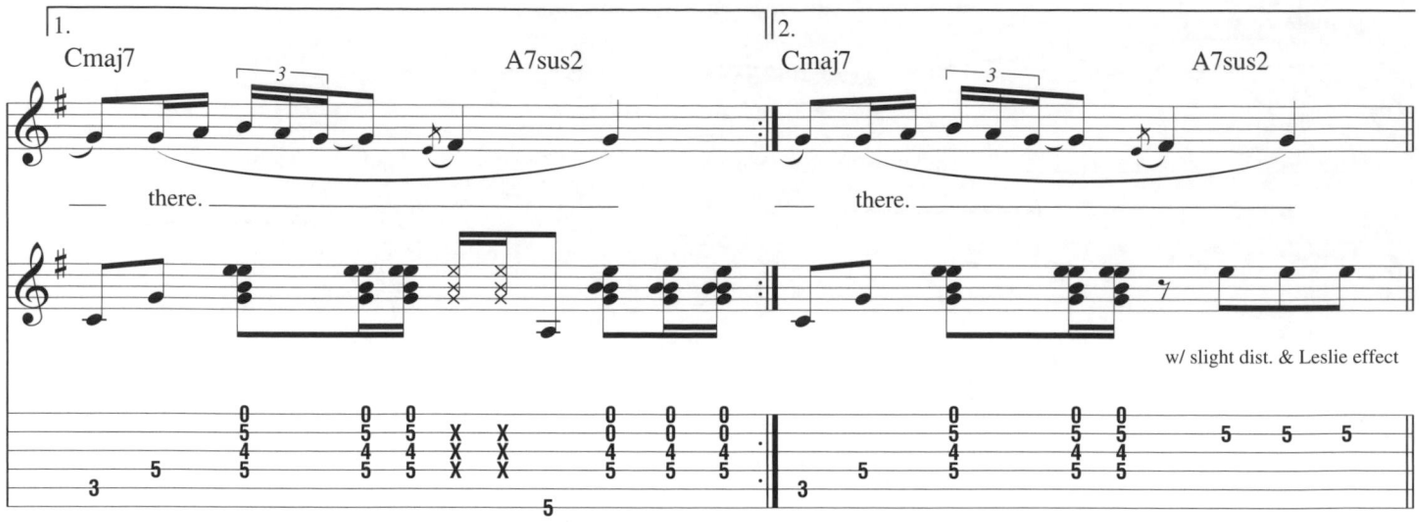
1.
Cmaj7
A7sus2
there.
2.
Cmaj7
A7sus2
there.
w/ slight dist. & Leslie effect

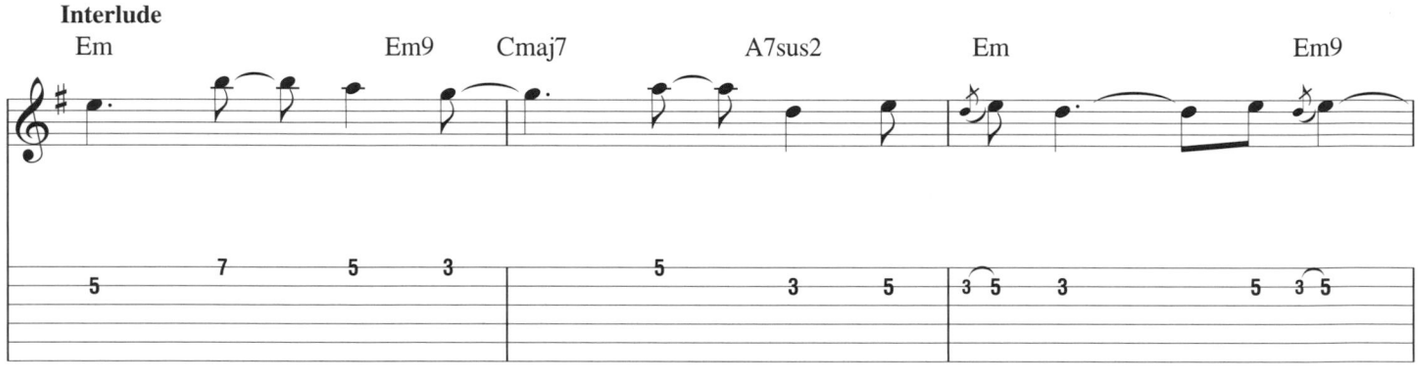
Interlude
Em
Em9
Cmaj7
A7sus2
Em
Em9

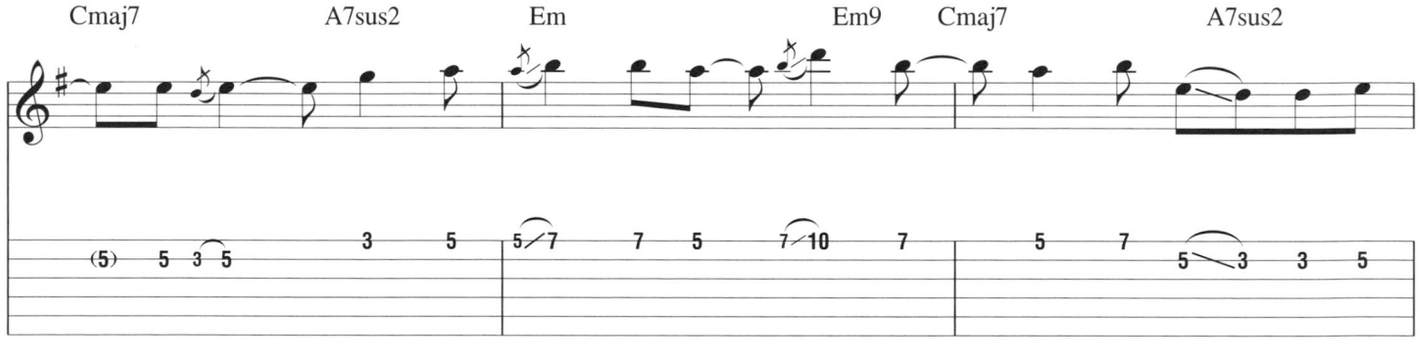
Cmaj7
A7sus2
Em
Em9
Cmaj7
A7sus2

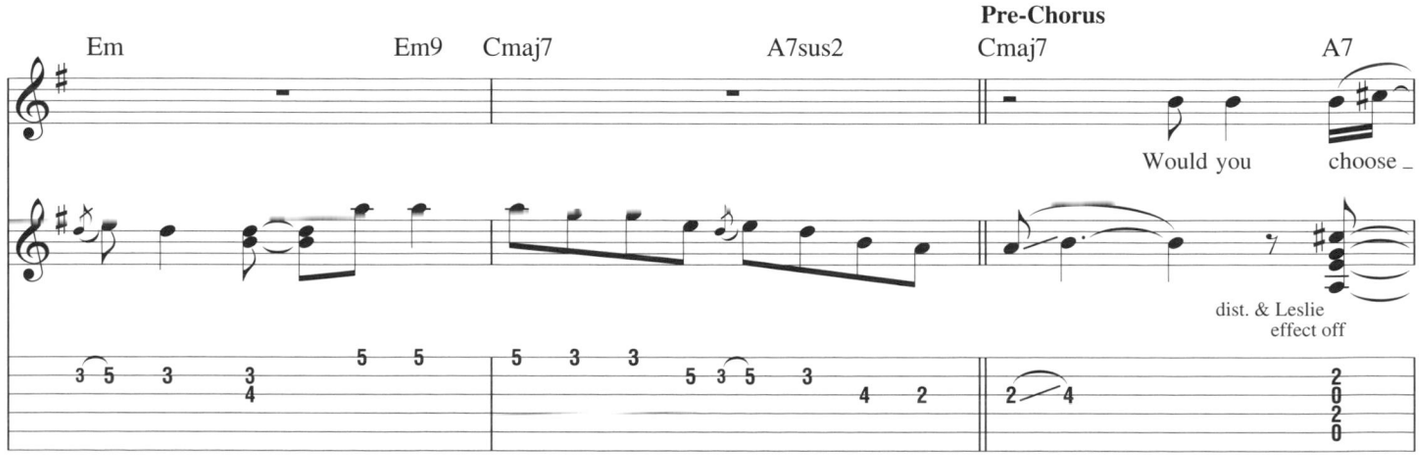
Em
Em9
Cmaj7
A7sus2
Pre-Chorus
Cmaj7
A7
Would you
choose
dist. & Leslie
effect off

A7sus2 A7 A7sus2 Cmaj7 A7
a, wa - ter o - ver wine?
Hold
D.S. al Coda
N.C.
the wheel and drive.
P.S.
Coda
Cmaj7 A7sus2
there.
Outro
Em Em9
Do, do, do,
Cmaj7 A7sus2 Em Em9
do, do, do, do, do, do, do.
No, no,

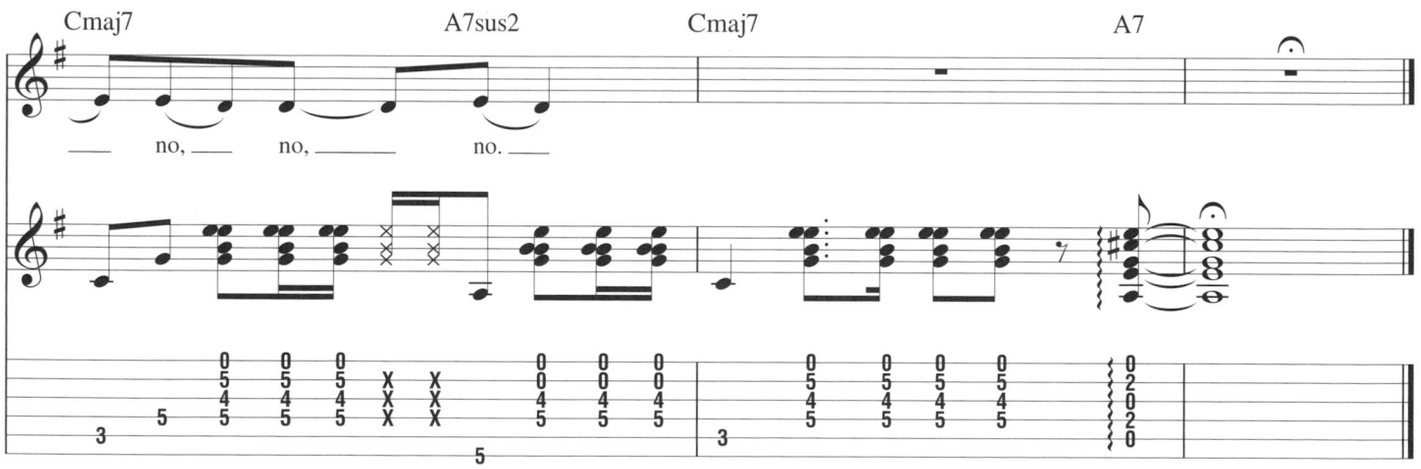

Additional Lyrics

2. So if I decide to waiver the
Chance to be one of the hive,
Will I choose water over wine
And hold my own and drive?
Oh, oh, oh.

Pre-Chorus It's driven me before,
And it seems to be the way,
That ev'ryone else gets around.
But lately I'm beginning to find
That when I drive myself my light is found,

IRIS
Goo Goo Dolls

Video Lesson – 20 minutes, 31 seconds

Tuning: (low to high) B–D–D–D–D–D
Key of D

Guitar Tone:

- acoustic guitar or clean tone electric
- light reverb

Chords:

Intro:

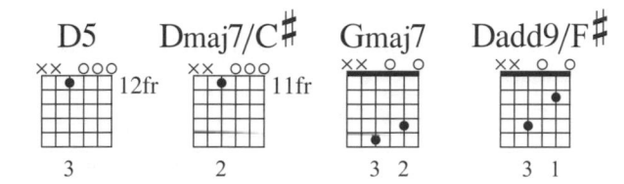

Verse:

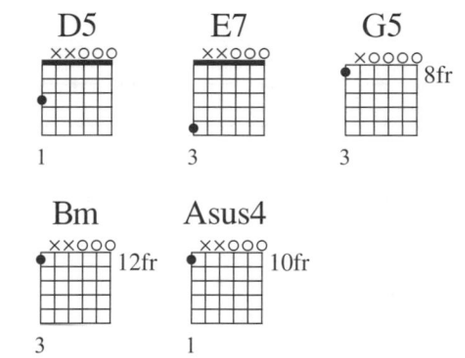

Interlude/Guitar Solo:

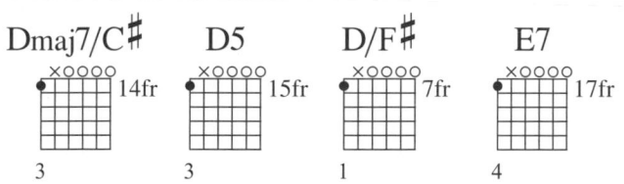

Techniques:

- Alternate Tuning: this song uses a very unique tuning. If you stick with your normal set of strings, be careful when fretting the strings that are tuned down. Use light pressure and make sure to not accidentally bend the now looser strings.
- Open-String Chords: all of the chords in this song involve a mixture of fretted notes and open strings. Make sure to fret these with the tips of your fret-hand fingers, allowing the open strings to ring clearly.
- Arpeggios: for the arpeggio section in the Verse, pick the first note with a downstroke and then catch the next three with an upstroke. Repeat this pattern for each new chord.
- Odd Time Signatures: the song moves from 8/8 to 12/8 and 6/8. Be sure to count or feel those meter changes.
- Muted Notes: when strumming the chords during the Guitar Solo, fret with a slightly flattened or angled finger, allowing the 5th string to be muted. Strum right through all six strings.

Iris

from the Motion Picture CITY OF ANGELS

Words and Music by John Rzeznik

Tuning:
(low to high) B♭-D♭-D-D♭-D♯-D

Intro

Moderately slow ♩. = 51

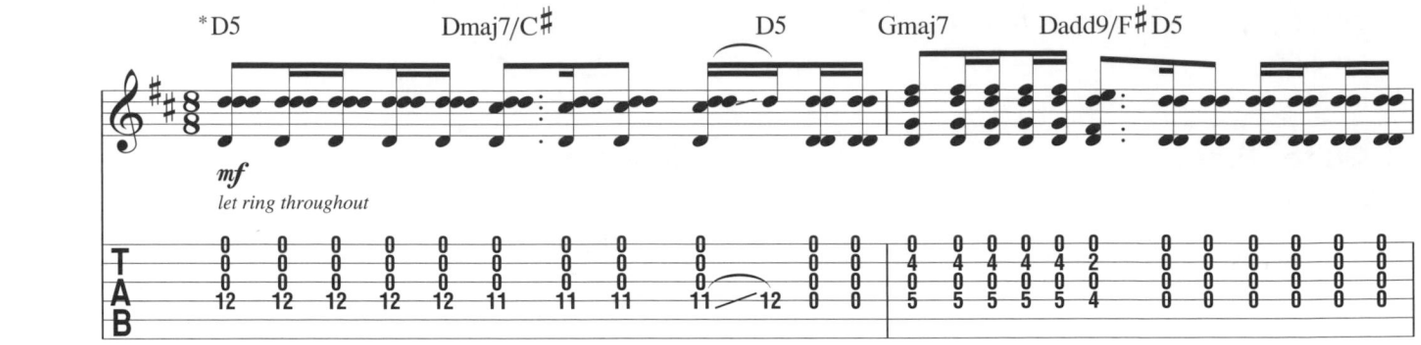

*Chord symbols reflect implied harmony.

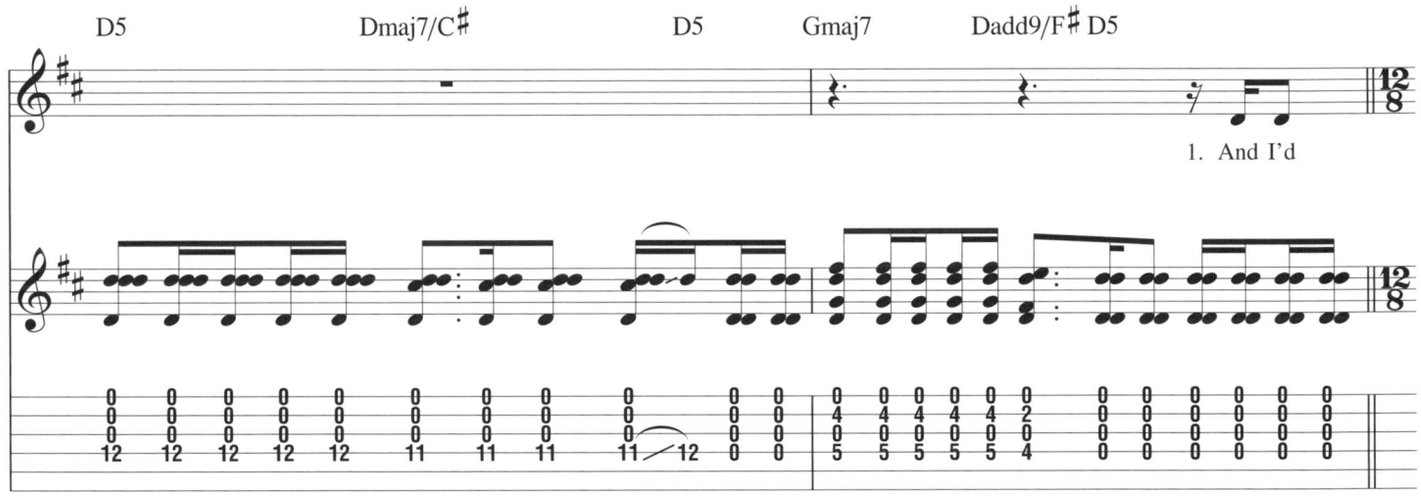

Verse

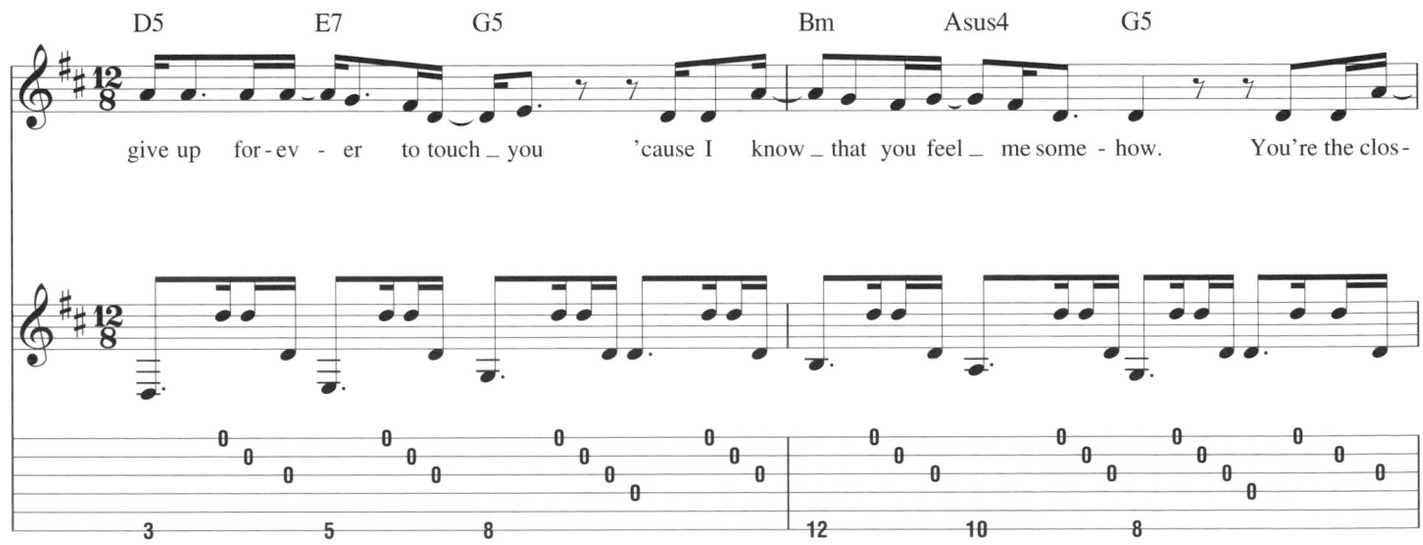

Copyright © 1998 BMG Platinum Songs and Scrap Metal Music
All Rights Administered by BMG Rights Management (US) LLC
All Rights Reserved Used by Permission

D5 E7 G5 Bm Asus4 G5
- est to heav - en that I'll ev-er be, and I don't wan-na go home right now. And all
3 5 8 12 10 8

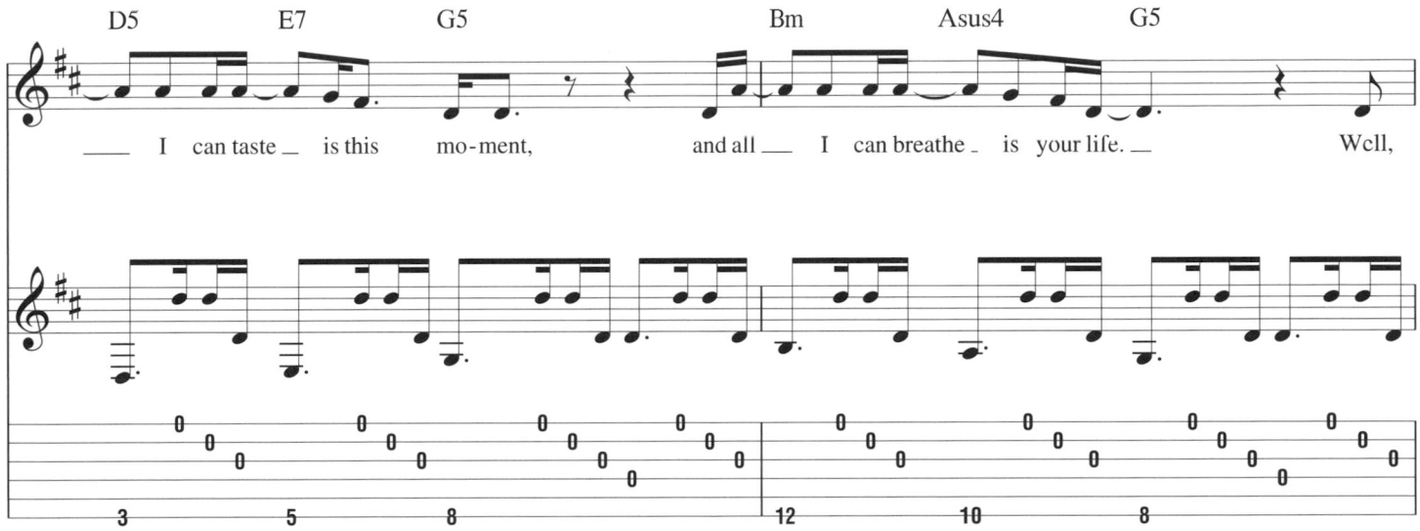
D5 E7 G5 Bm Asus4 G5
I can taste is this mo-ment, and all I can breathe is your life. Well,
3 5 8 12 10 8

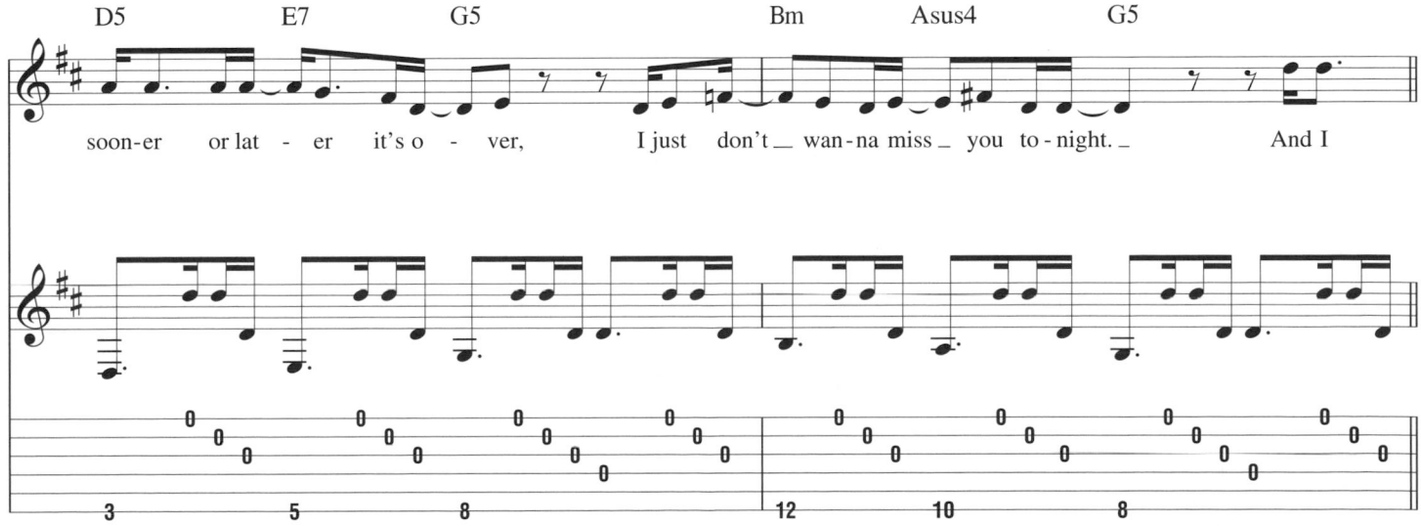
D5 E7 G5 Bm Asus4 G5
soon-er or lat - er it's o - ver, I just don't wan-na miss you to-night. And I
3 5 8 12 10 8

Chorus
Bm
Asus4
G5
don't want the world to see me 'cause I don't
Bm
Asus4
G5
think that they'd un - der - stand. When
Bm
Asus4
G5
ev - 'ry - thing's made to be bro - ken, I just want

To Coda 1
To Coda 2
Bm
Asus4
G5
you to know who I am.
Interlude
D5
Dmaj7/C♯
D5
Gmaj7
Dadd9/F♯ D5
D5
Dmaj7/C♯
D5
Gmaj7
Dadd9/F♯D5
2. And you can't

D.S. al Coda 1

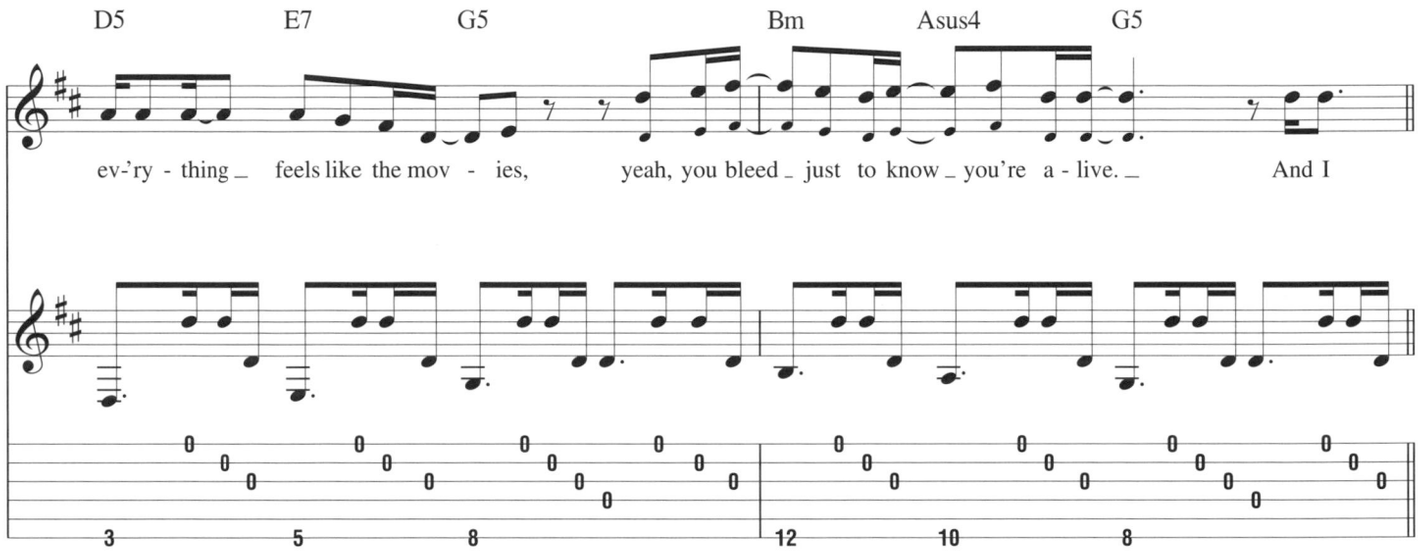

Coda 1

Interlude

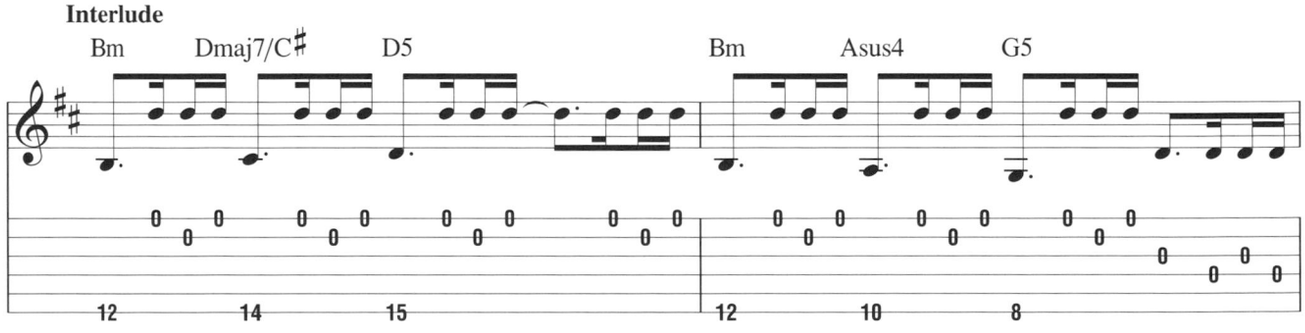

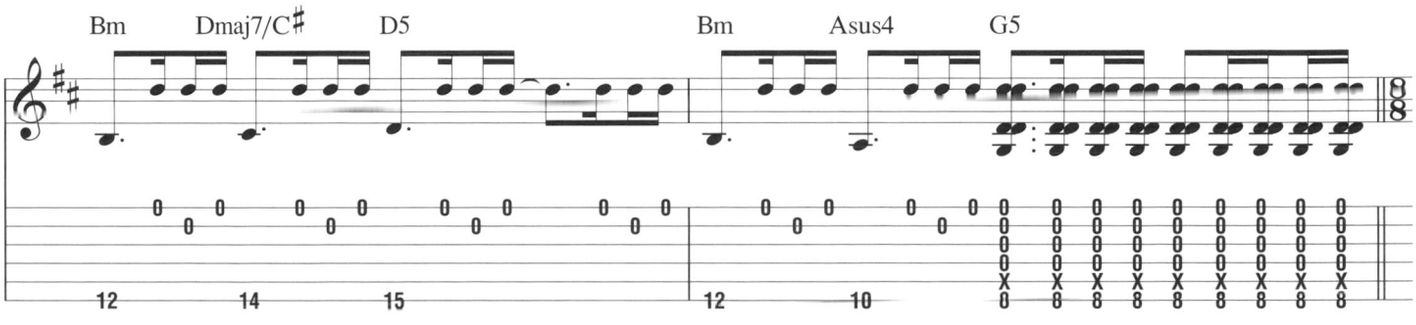

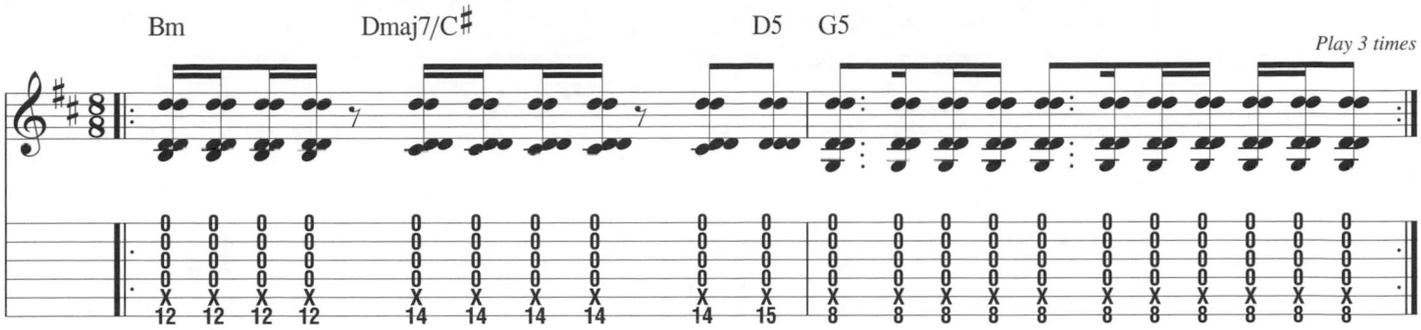

Guitar Solo

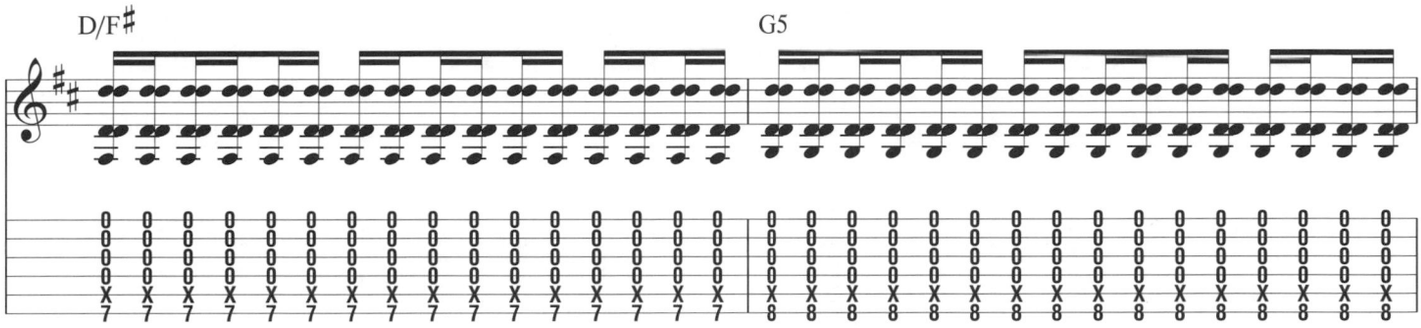

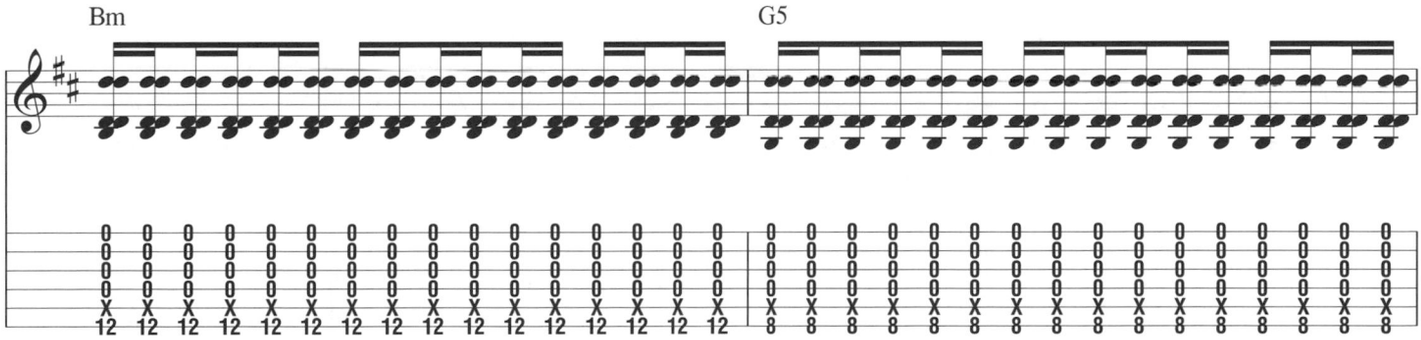

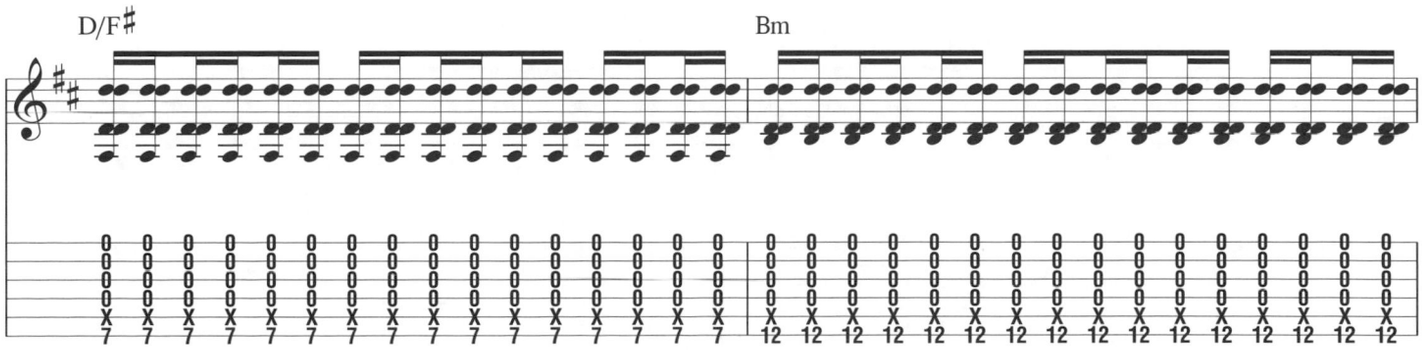

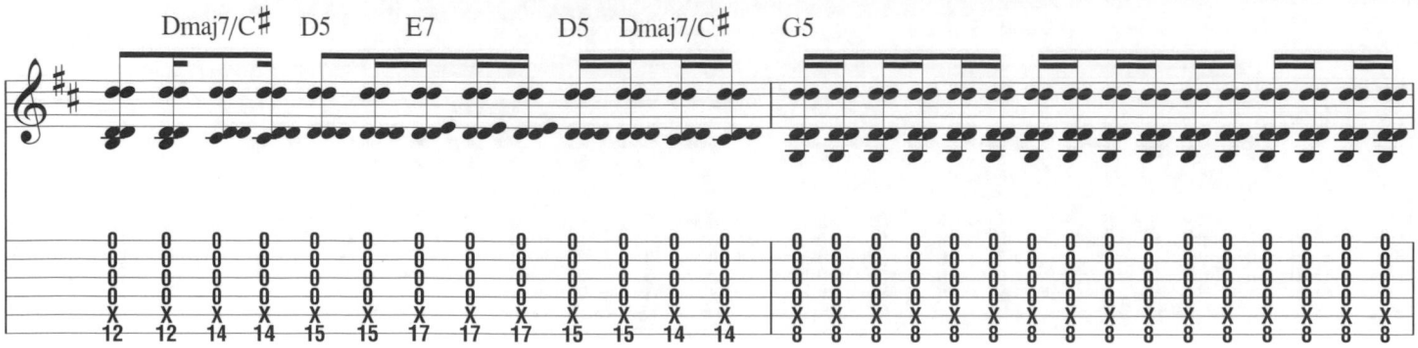
Dmaj7/C♯ D5 E7 D5 Dmaj7/C♯ G5
12 12 14 14 15 15 17 17 17 15 15 14 14
8 8 8 8 8 8 8 8 8 8 8 8 8 8 8

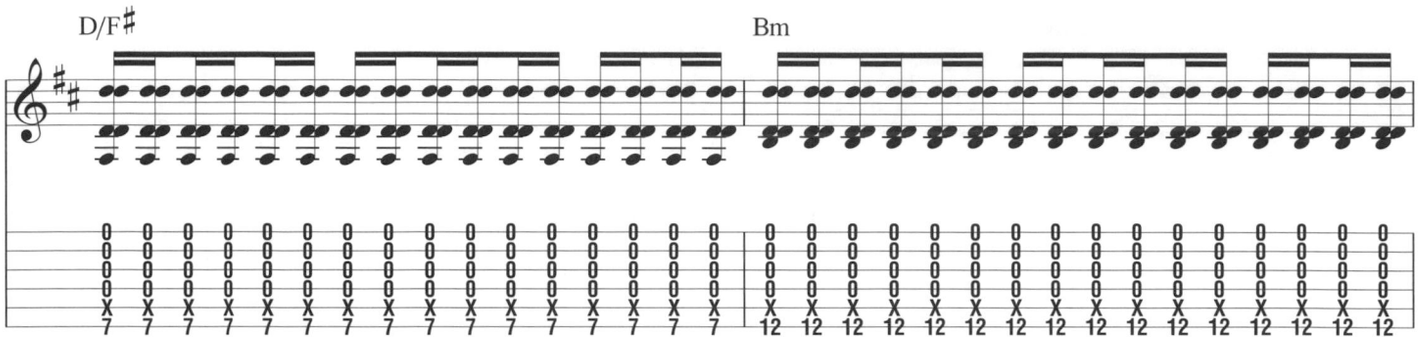
D/F♯ Bm
7 7 7 7 7 7 7 7 7 7 7 7 7 7 7
12 12 12 12 12 12 12 12 12 12 12 12 12 12 12

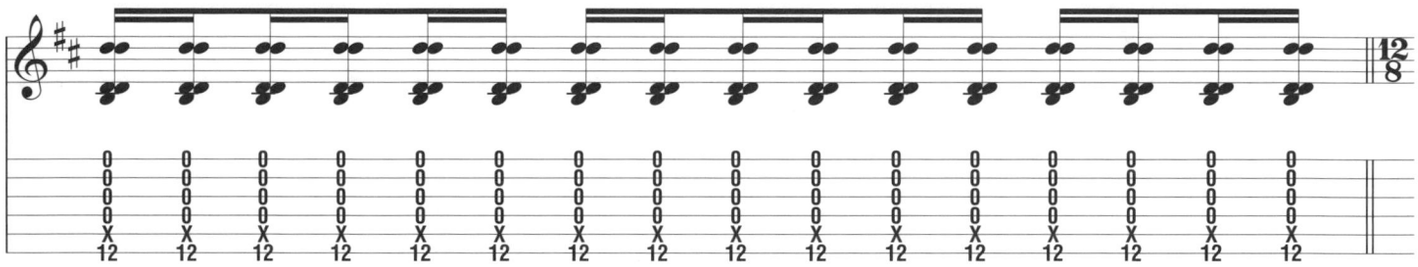
12 12 12 12 12 12 12 12 12 12 12 12 12 12 12

Interlude

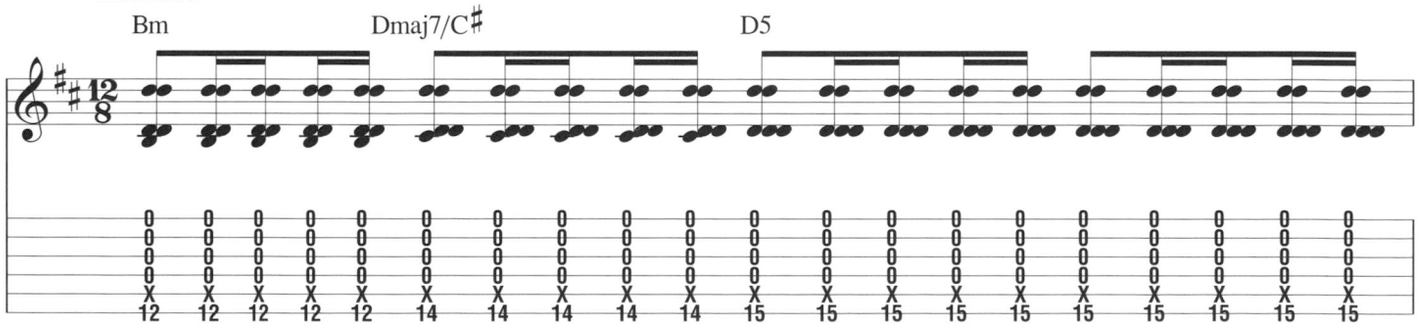
Bm Dmaj7/C♯ D5
12 12 12 12 12 14 14 14 14 14 15 15 15 15 15 15 15 15 15 15

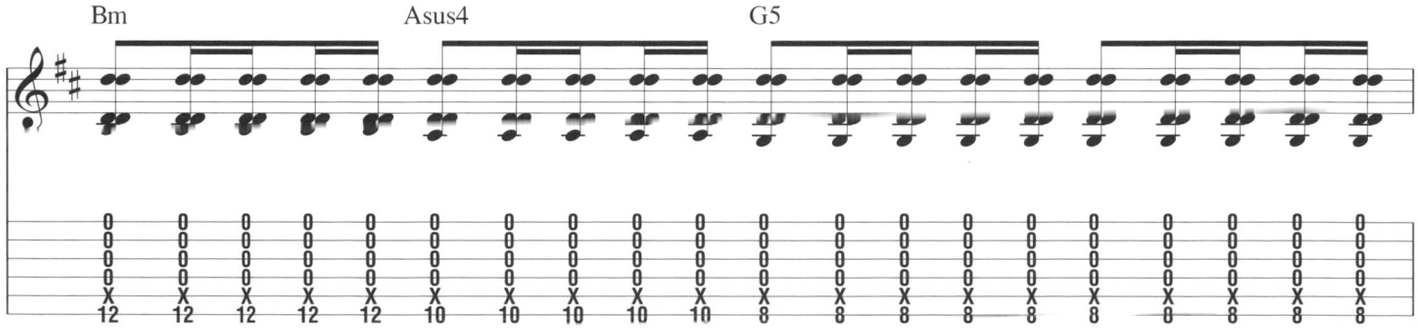
Bm Asus4 G5
12 12 12 12 12 10 10 10 10 10 8 8 8 8 8 8 8 8 8

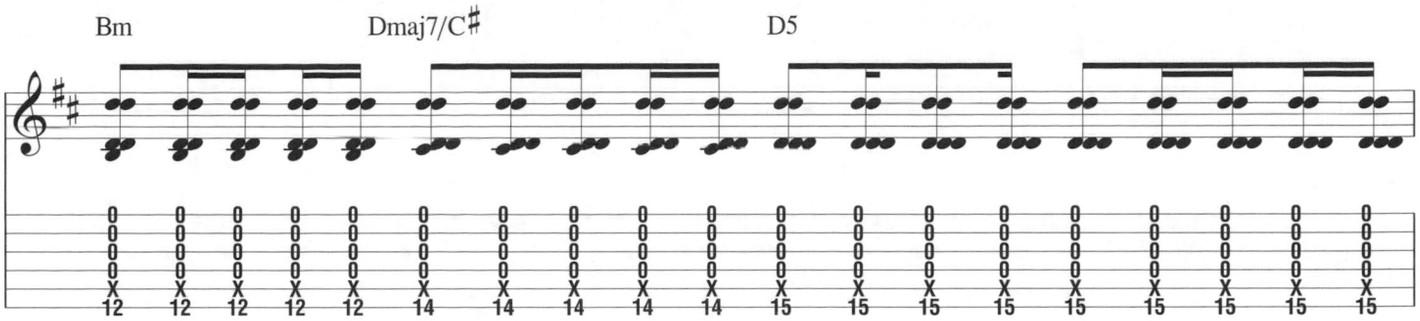
Bm
Dmaj7/C♯
D5

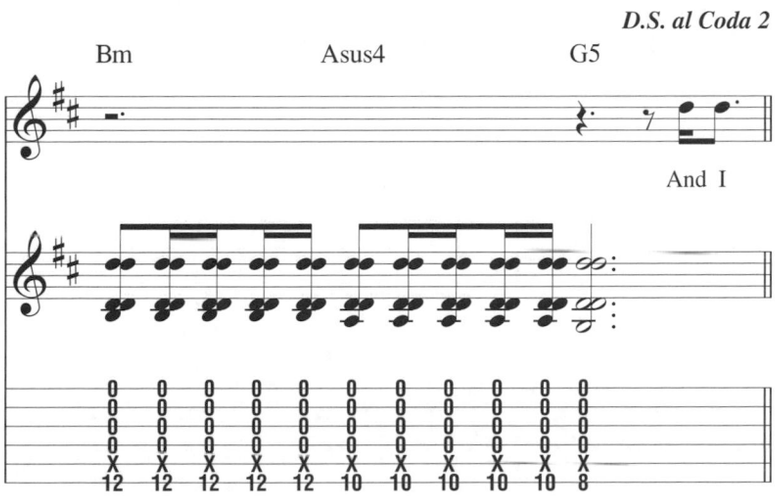
D.S. al Coda 2
Bm
Asus4
G5
And I

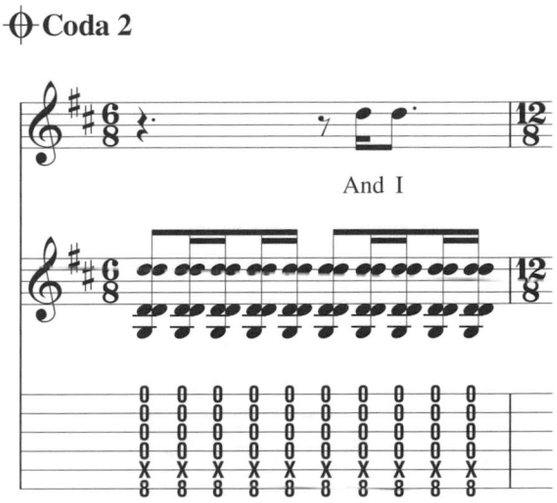
Coda 2
And I

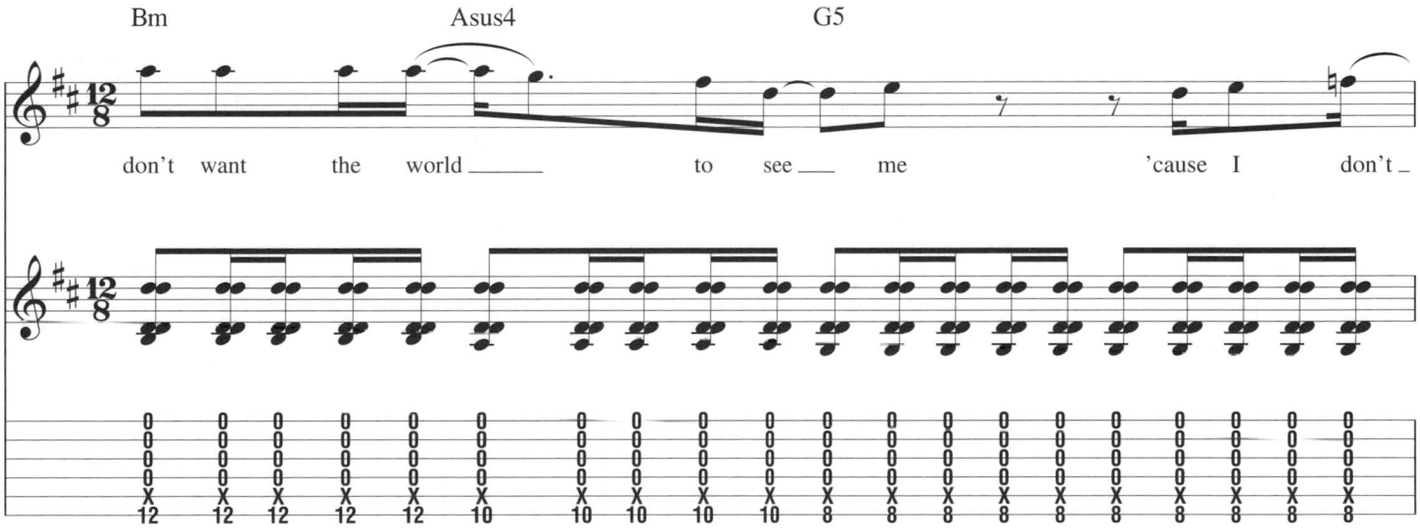
Bm
Asus4
G5
don't want the world to see me 'cause I don't

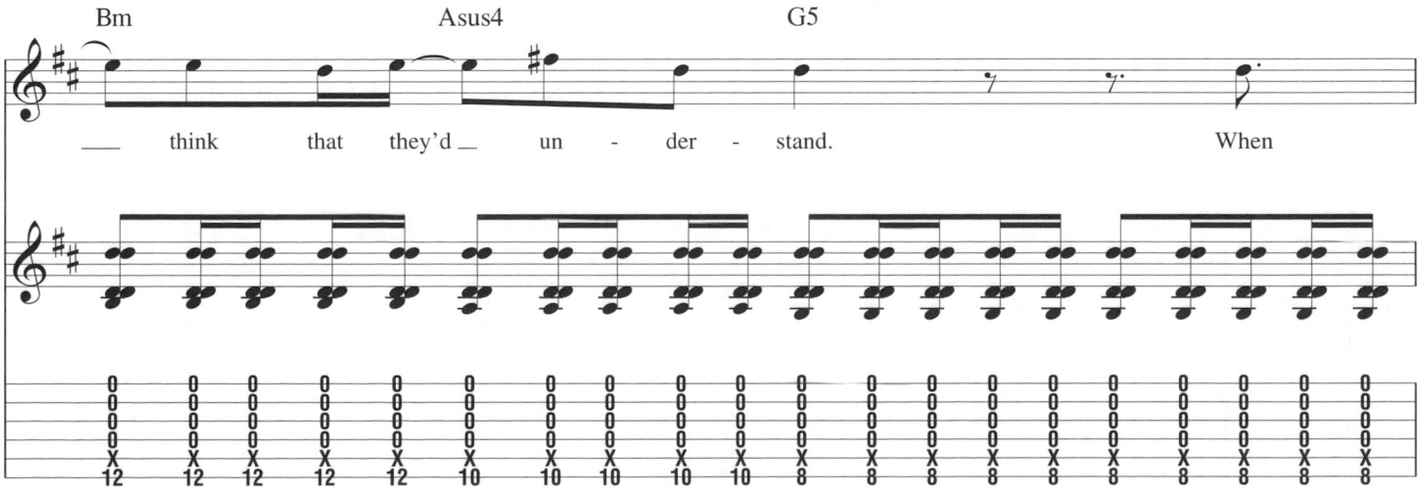
Bm
Asus4
G5
think that they'd un - der - stand. When

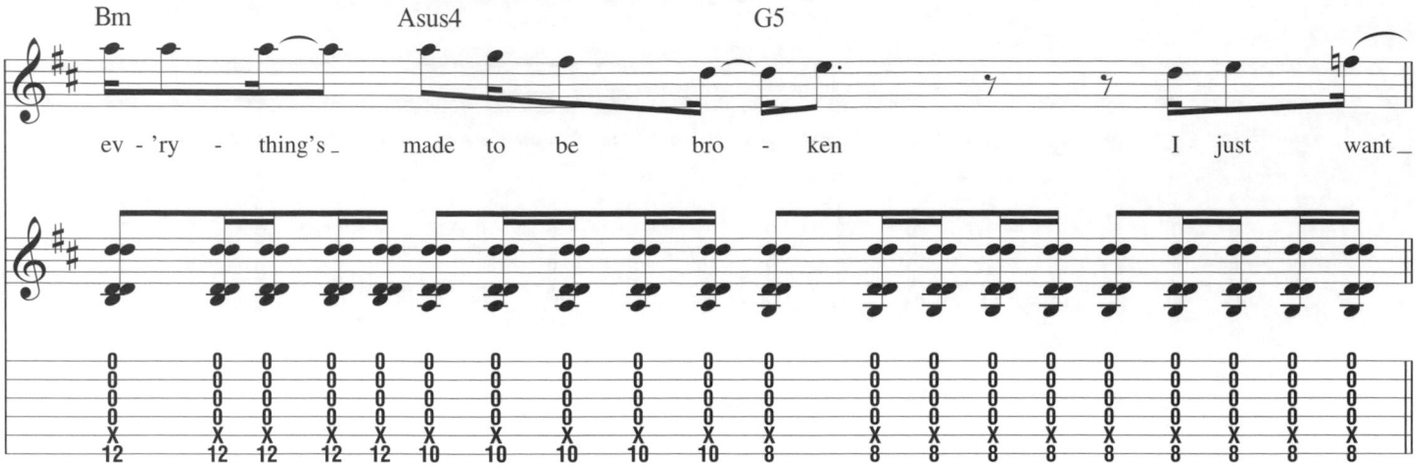

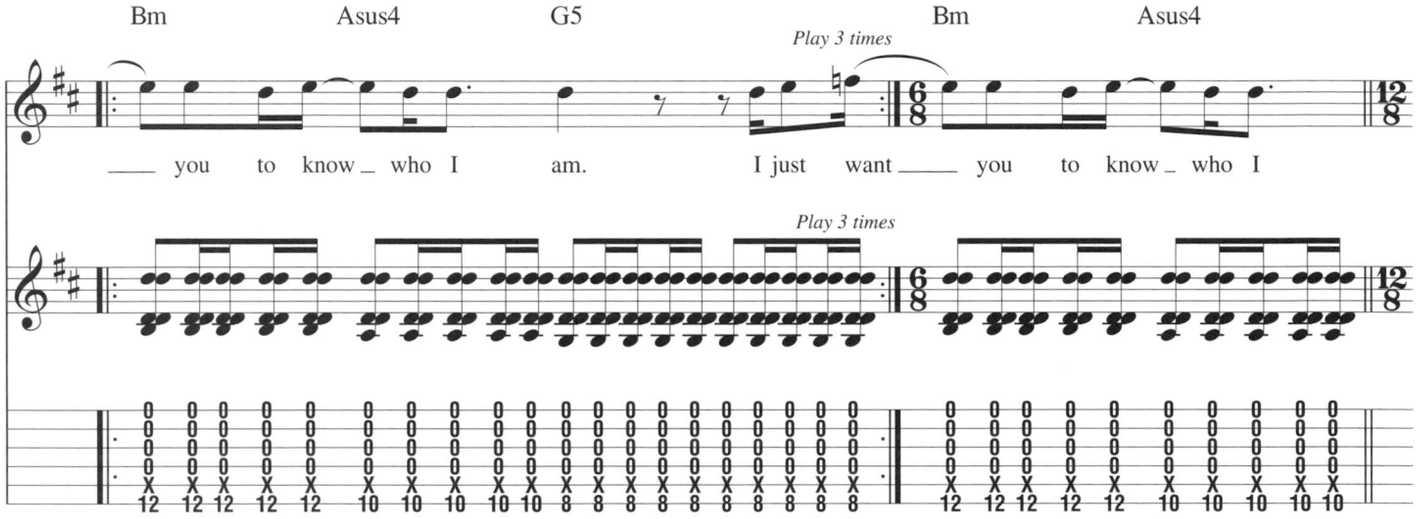

Outro

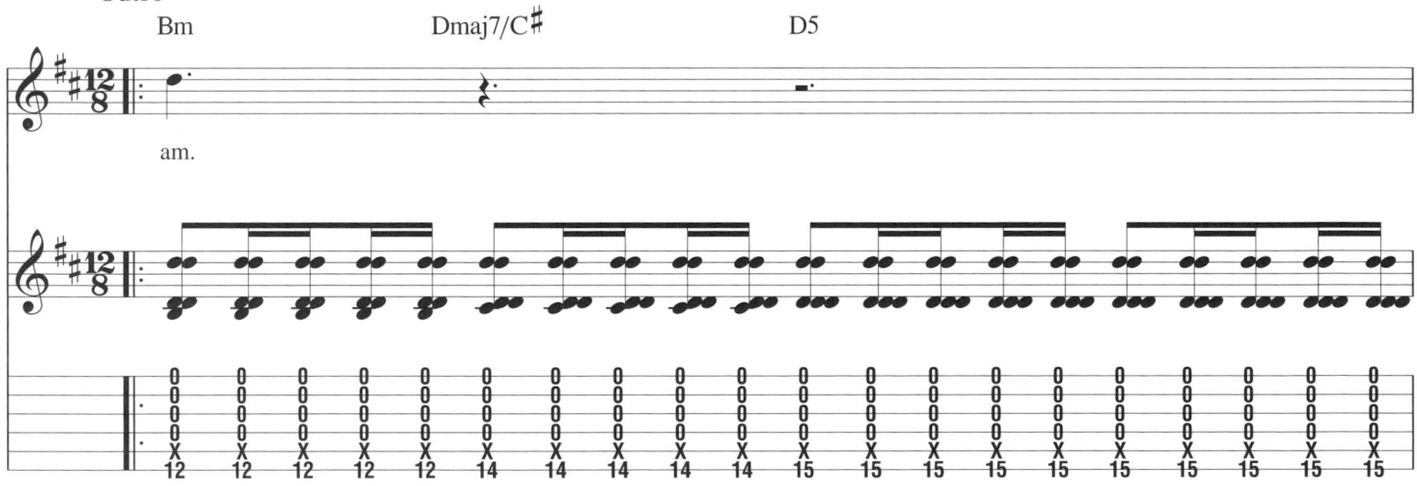

Repeat and fade

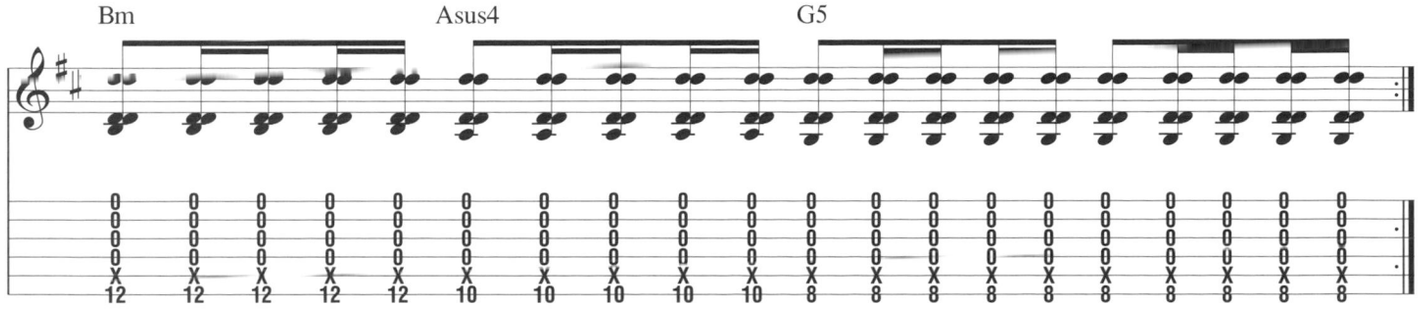

LAYLA (UNPLUGGED)

Eric Clapton

Video Lesson – 17 minutes, 32 seconds

Standard Tuning: (low to high) E–A–D–G–B–E
Key of D minor, C♯ minor

Guitar Tone:

- acoustic guitar or clean tone electric
- light reverb

Chords:

Intro:

Verse:

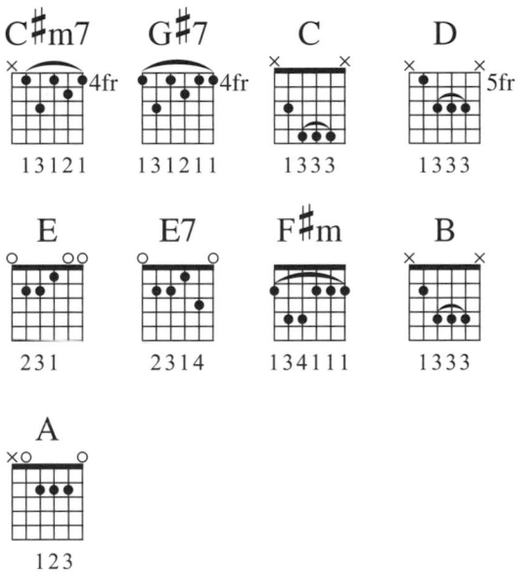

Scales/Arpeggios:

Guitar Solos:

D Minor Pentatonic Scale

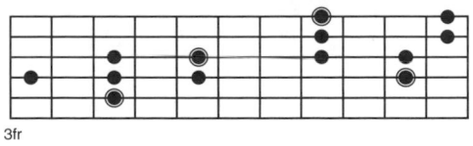

Techniques:

- Hammer-Ons/Pull-Offs: for hammer-ons, strike the first note and then come down forcefully with your fret-hand finger to sound the next note. For the pull-off, strike the first note while also fretting the second note below. Pull off in a slightly downward motion, allowing the second note to ring. Be careful not to sound the higher string with your pull-off finger.
- Vibrato: Clapton is a master of vibrato. Shake the note up and down, creating a little series of quick bends and releases. Vary the intensity and speed of the vibrato in accordance to the phrasing of the solo. Be sure to keep your wrist loose!
- Barre Chords: keep your 1st finger straight and flat and make sure all fretted notes ring clearly. You might find it helpful to roll your 1st finger a bit to the outside (towards the thumb) to help it remain flat.
- String Bending: bending on an acoustic can be tough! Make sure you use support fingers behind the fretted note.

Layla

Words and Music by Eric Clapton and Jim Gordon

Copyright © 1970 by Eric Patrick Clapton
Copyright Renewed
International Copyright Secured All Rights Reserved

Verse
C♯m7
G♯7
C♯m7
C
D
1. What will you do when you get lone - ly?
No one wait-ing by your
side.
You've been run - nin',
hid - in' much too long.
E
E7
F♯m
B
E
A
F♯m
B
E
A
Chorus
D5
B♭5
You know it's just your fool - ish pride.
Lay - la,
C5
D5
B♭5
C5
D5
got me on my knees. Lay - la,
beg - gin' dar - lin', please. Lay - la,

B♭5
C5
D5
B♭5
dar - lin' won't you ease my wor - ried mind?

Verse
C5
N.C.(A)
(C)
C♯m7
G♯7
2. Tried to give you con - so - la - tion,
3. See additional lyrics

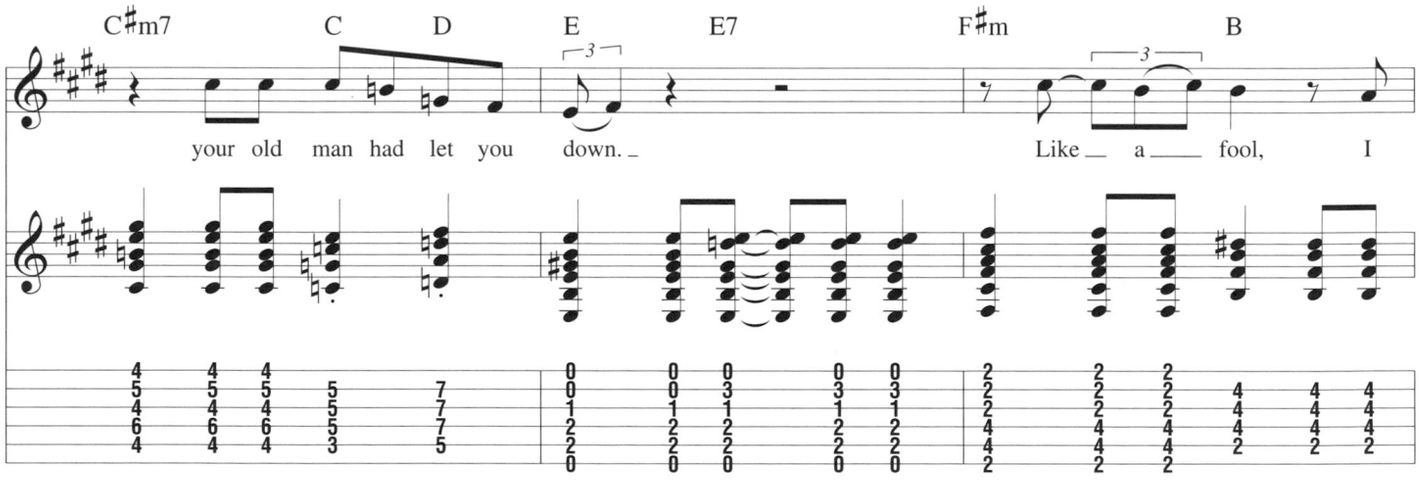
C♯m7
C
D
E
E7
F♯m
B
your old man had let you down.
Like a fool, I

E
A
F♯m
B
E
A
fell in love with you.
You turned my whole world up - side down.
Lay - la,

Chorus
D5 B♭5 C5 D5 B♭5
got me on my knees. Lay - la,
C5 D5 B♭5 C5 D5
To Coda
beg - gin' dar - lin', please. Lay - la,
dar - lin', won't you ease my wor - ried
1. B♭5 C5 N.C.(A) (C)
mind?
2. B♭5
mind?
C5 D5 B♭5 C5 D5
Lay - la,
got me on my knees. Lay - la,

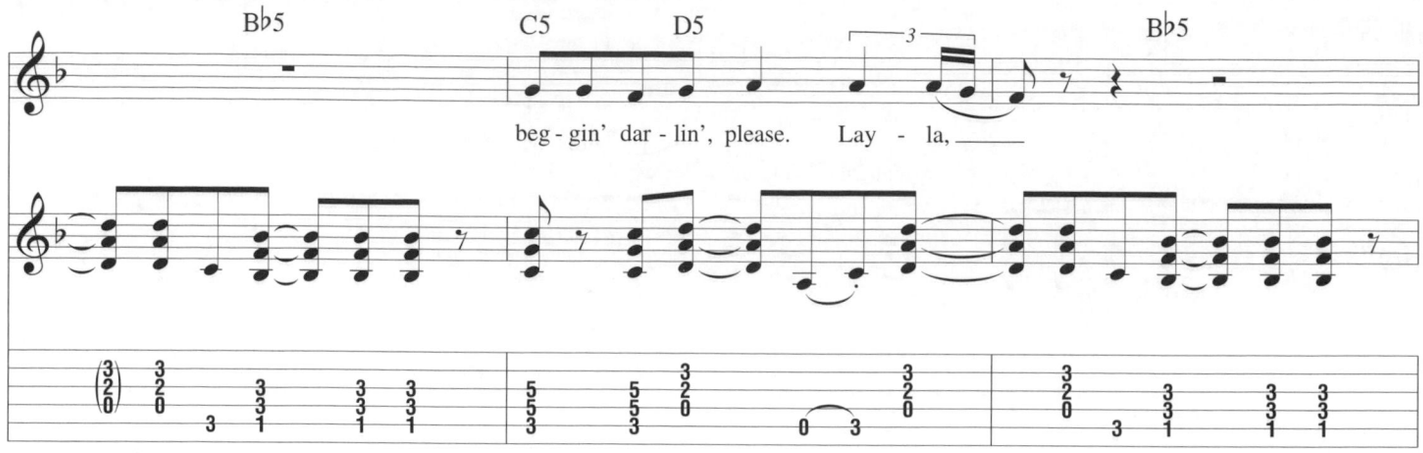
B♭5
C5
D5
B♭5
beg - gin' dar - lin', please. Lay - la,

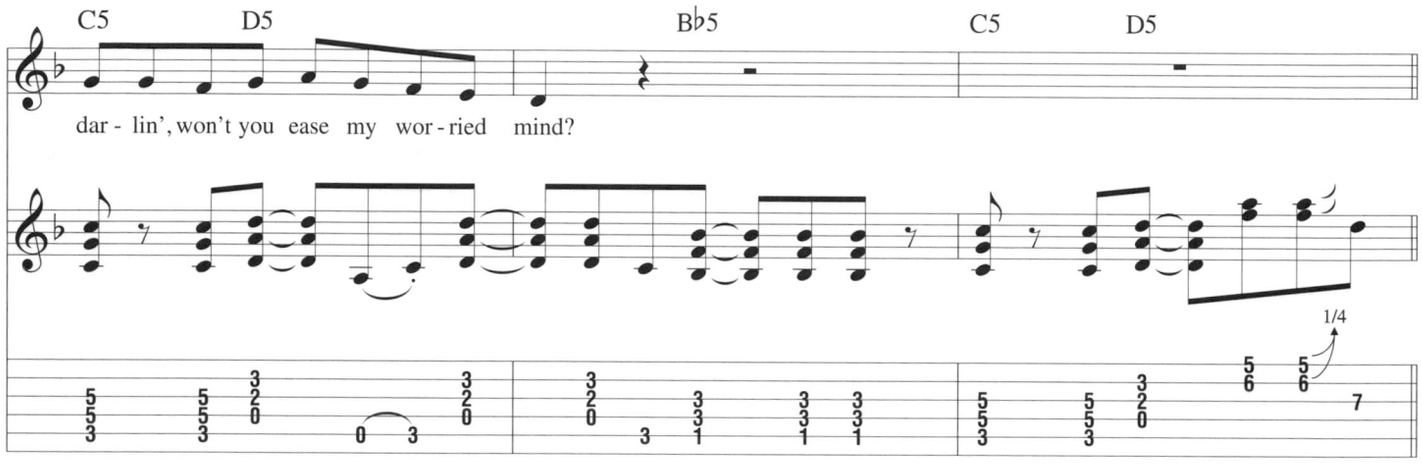
C5
D5
B♭5
C5
D5
dar - lin', won't you ease my wor - ried mind?
1/4

Guitar Solo

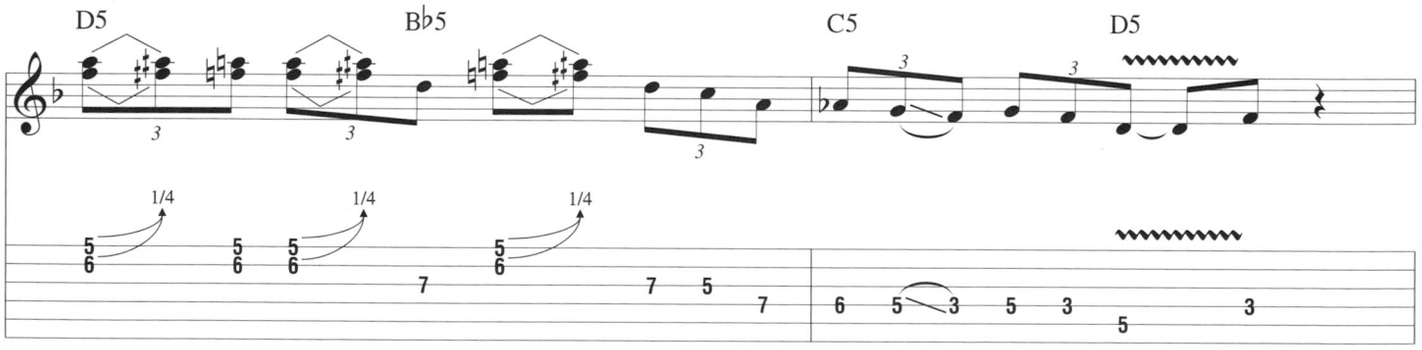
D5
B♭5
C5
D5
1/4
1/4
1/4

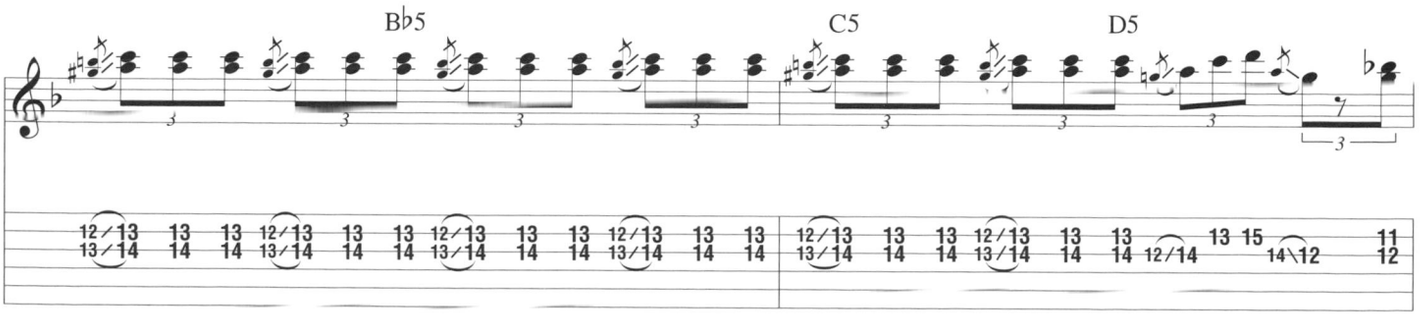
B♭5
C5
D5

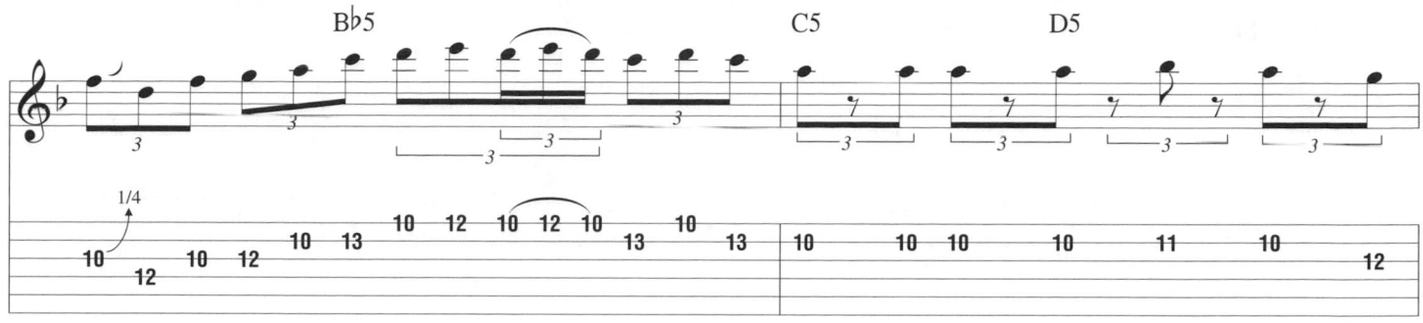
B♭5
C5
D5
1/4

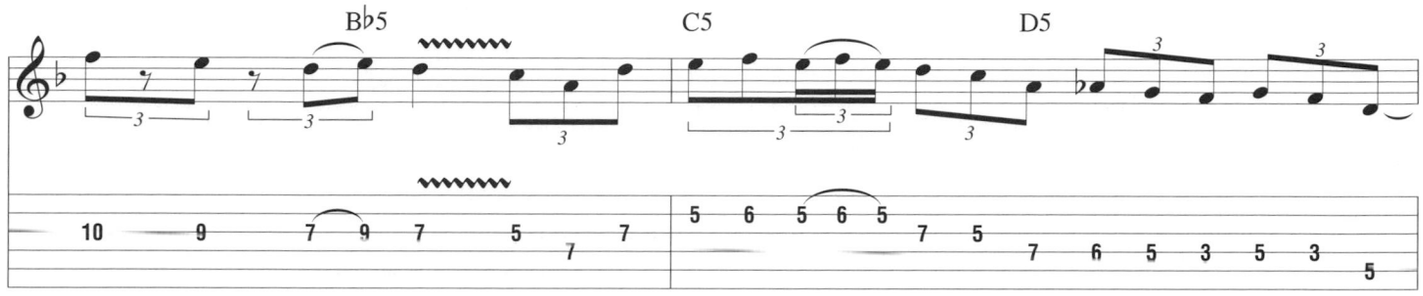
B♭5
C5
D5

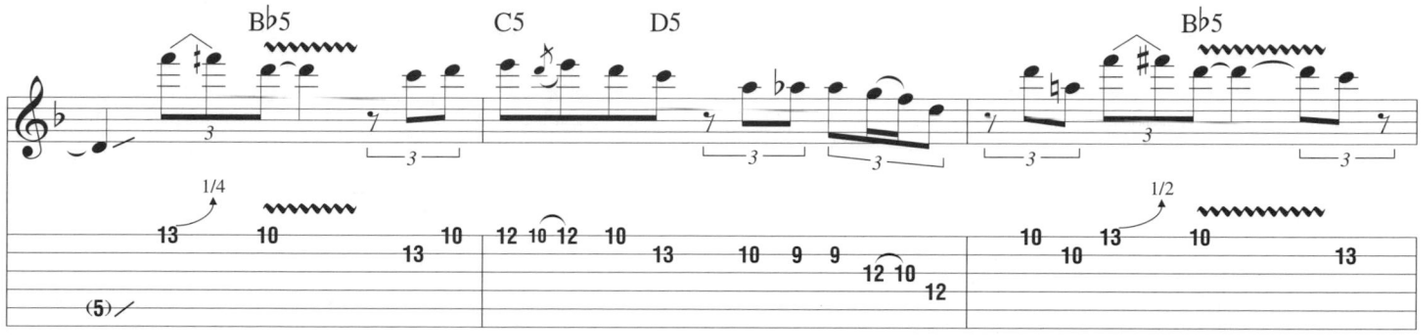
B♭5
C5
D5
B♭5
1/4
1/2

C5
D5
B♭5
C5
D5
1/2

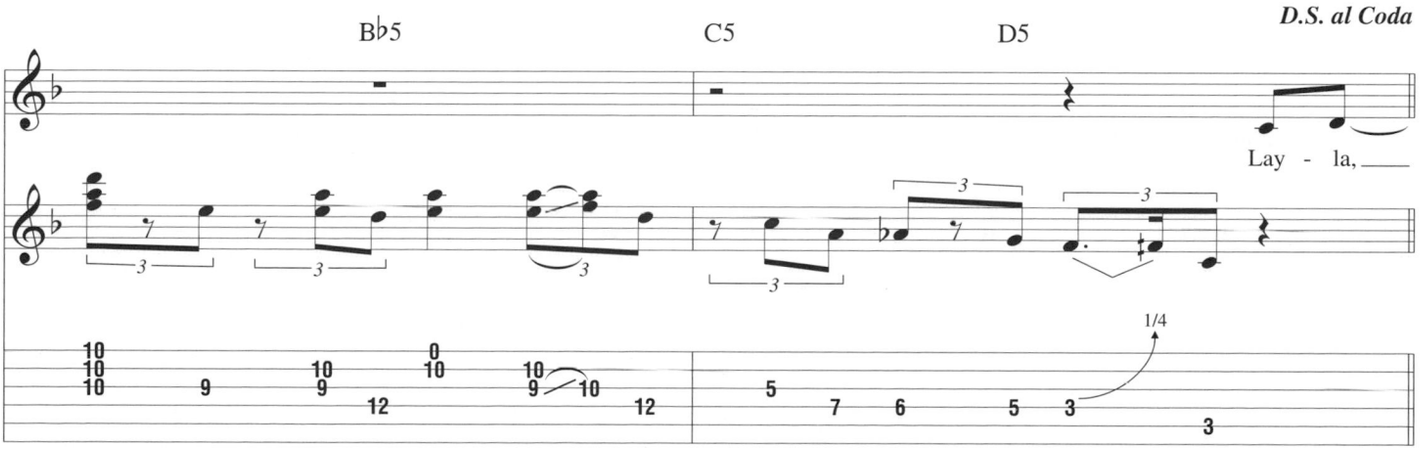
D.S. al Coda
B♭5
C5
D5
Lay - la,
1/4

Additional Lyrics

3. Make the best of the situation,
Before I fin'ly go insane.
Please don't say we'll never find a way.
Tell me all my love's in vain.

MR. JONES
Counting Crows

Video Lesson – 9 minutes, 5 seconds

Standard Tuning: (low to high) E–A–D–G–B–E
Key of A minor, C

Guitar Tone:

- acoustic guitar or clean tone electric
- light reverb

Chords:

Intro/Verse:

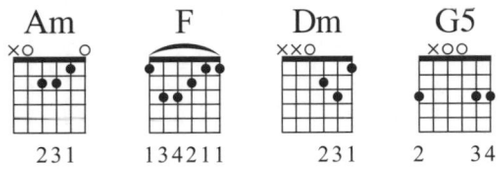

Chorus:

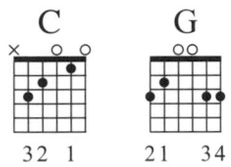

Bridge:

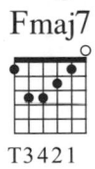

Techniques:

- Open-Position Chords: make sure all the open strings ring clearly. If not, you might need to fret more on your fingertips so you aren't unintentionally muting any strings.
- Barre Chords: keep your 1st finger straight and flat and make sure all fretted notes ring clearly. You might find it helpful to roll your 1st finger a bit to the outside (towards the thumb) to help it remain flat.
- Thumb-Fretting: for the Fmaj7 chord in the Bridge, fret the low F on the 6th string with the side of your fret-hand thumb. You may have to adjust your normal fret-hand position to make this comfortable.
- Muted Strums: keep your fret hand lightly in contact with the strings, being careful not to accidentally fret any notes by pressing down too hard. Strum the muted strings, producing a "click" type sound. You can also assist the damping by using your pick hand to palm mute the strings near the bridge.

Mr. Jones

Words and Music by Adam Duritz, David Bryson, Charles Gillingham, Matthew Malley, Steve Bowman, Daniel Vickrey and Ben Mize

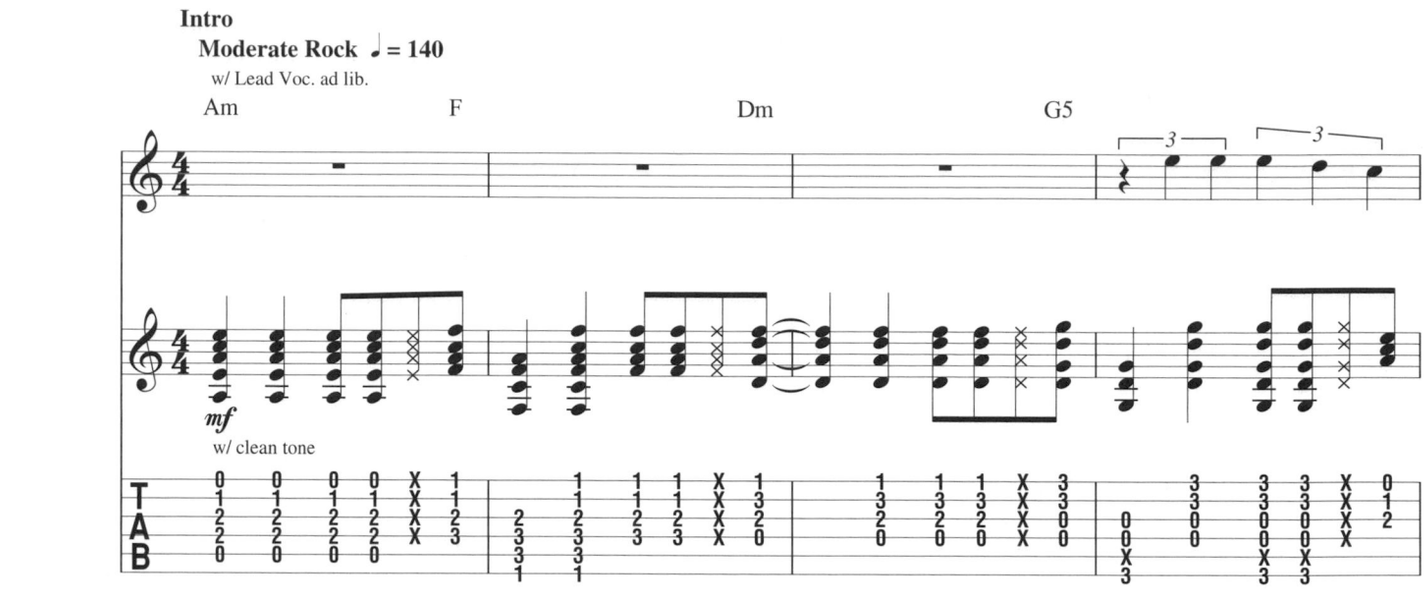

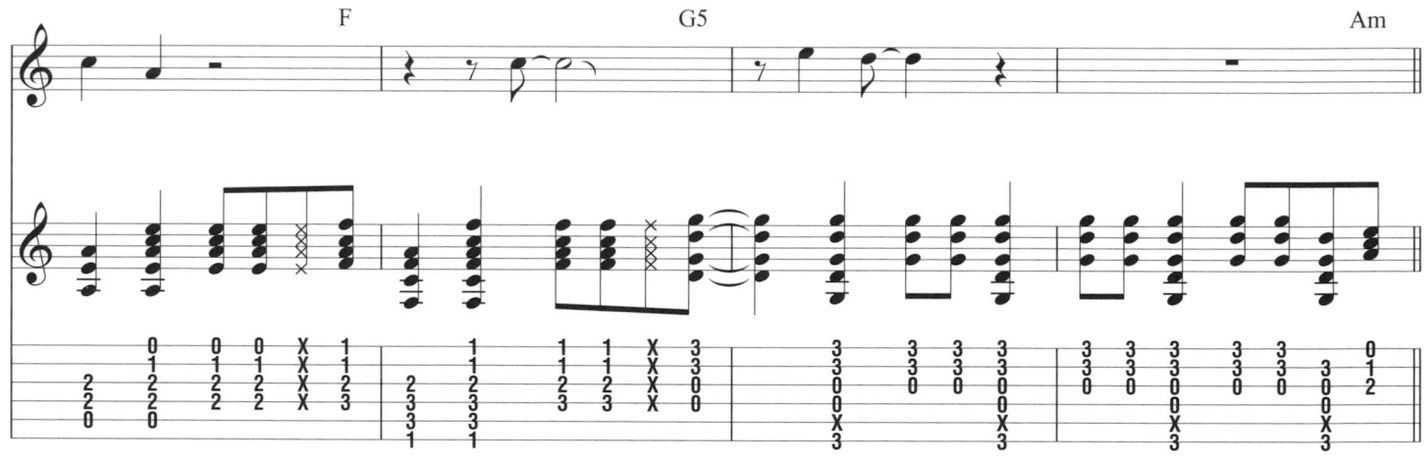

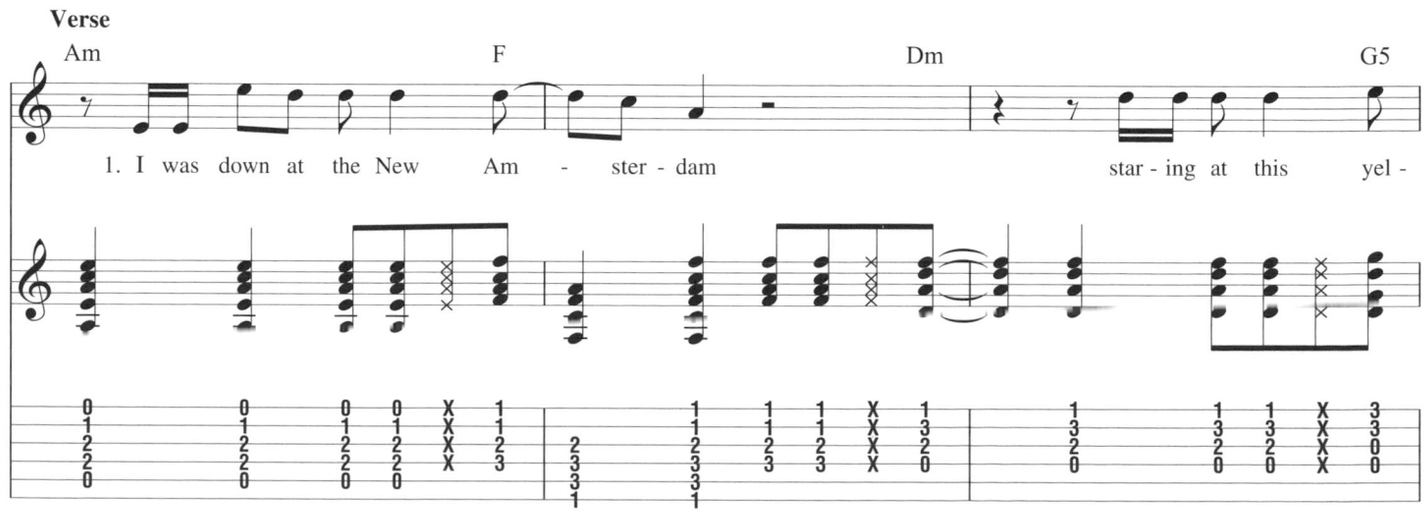

Copyright © 1993 Jones Falls Music
All Rights Administered by Atlas Music Publishing
All Rights Reserved Used by Permission

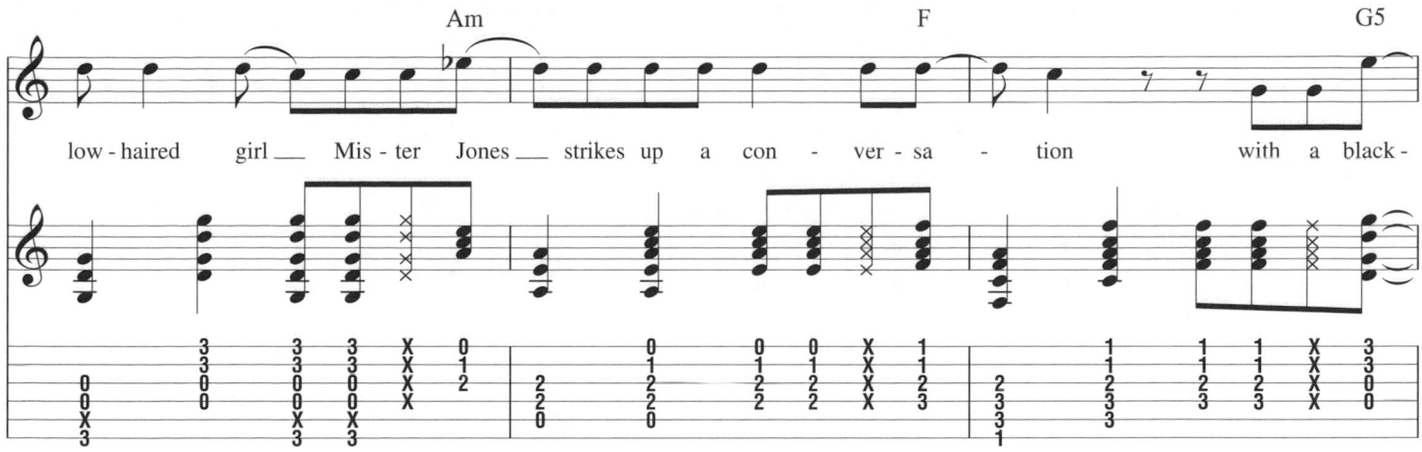
Am
F
G5
low - haired girl Mis - ter Jones strikes up a con - ver - sa - tion with a black -

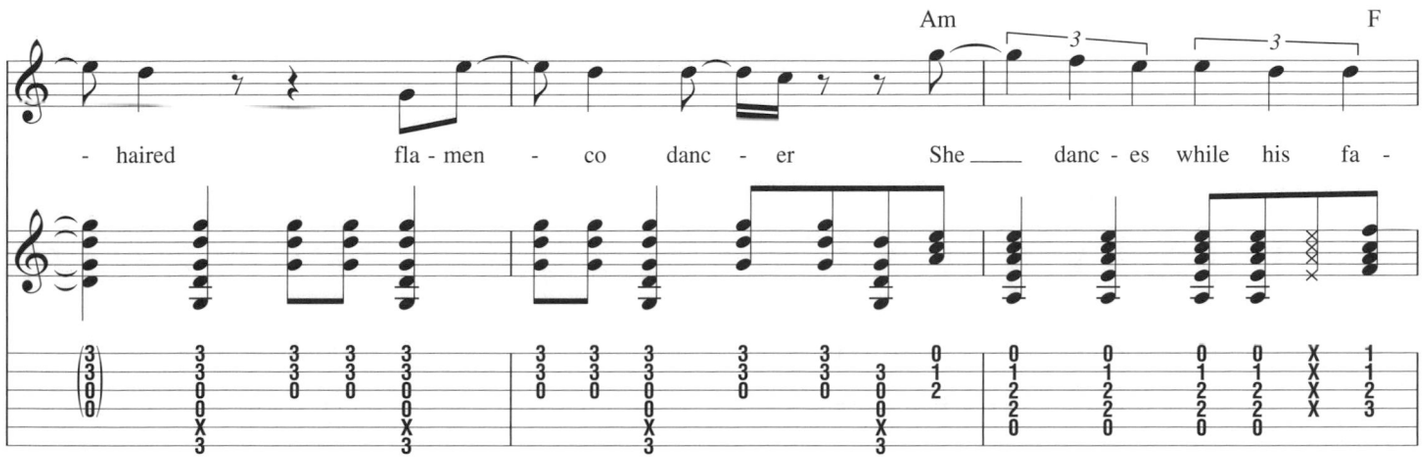
Am
F
- haired fla - men - co danc - er She danc - es while his fa -

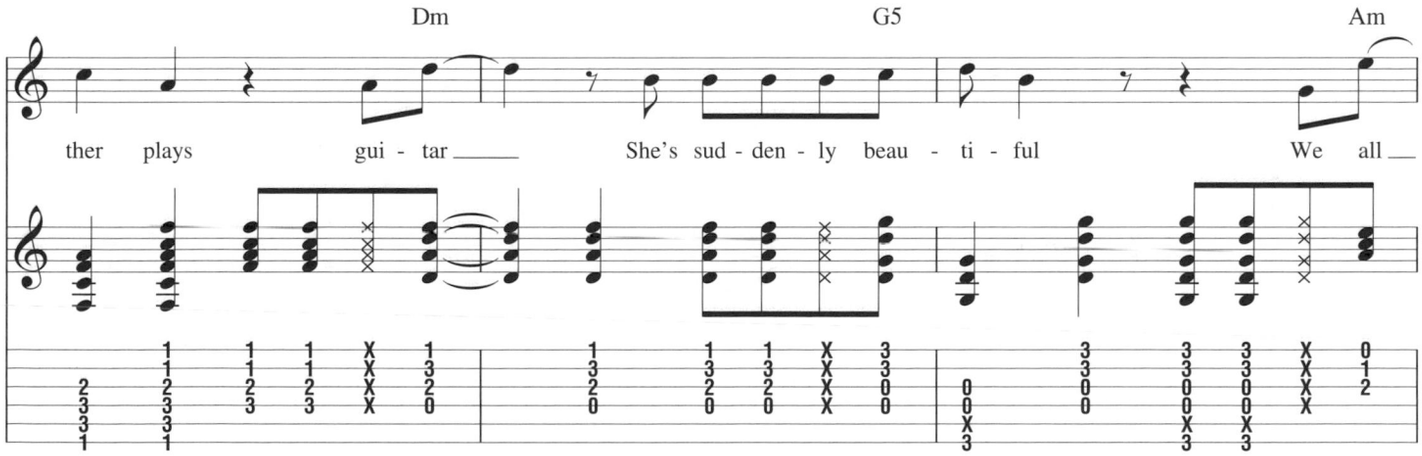
Dm
G5
Am
ther plays gui - tar She's sud - den - ly beau - ti - ful We all

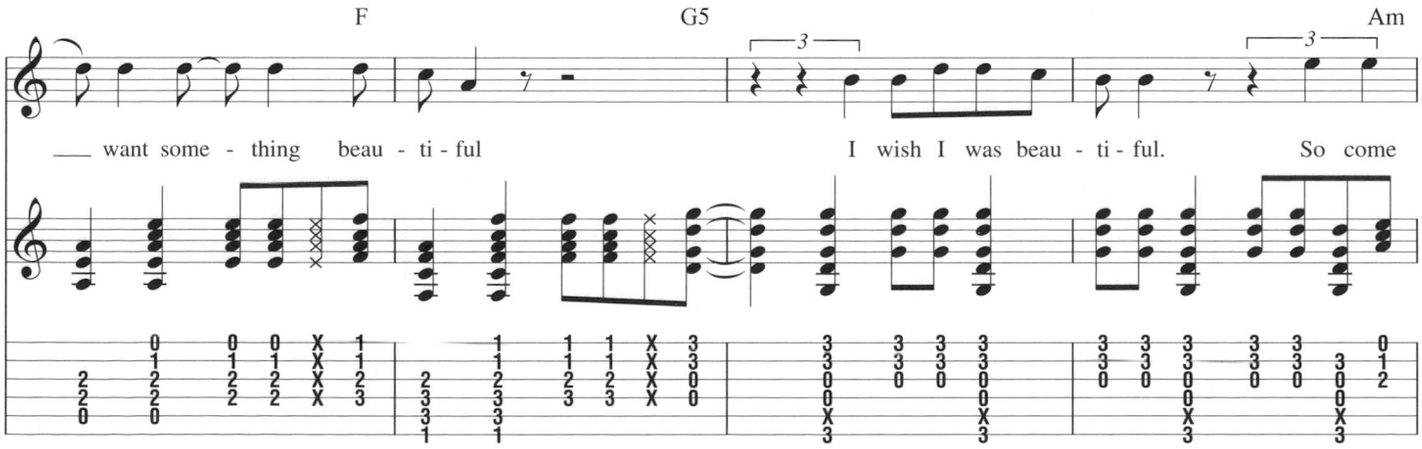
F
G5
Am
want some - thing beau - ti - ful I wish I was beau - ti - ful. So come

w/ Lead Voc. ad lib.
F
Dm
G5
Am
dance this si - lence down through the morn - ing

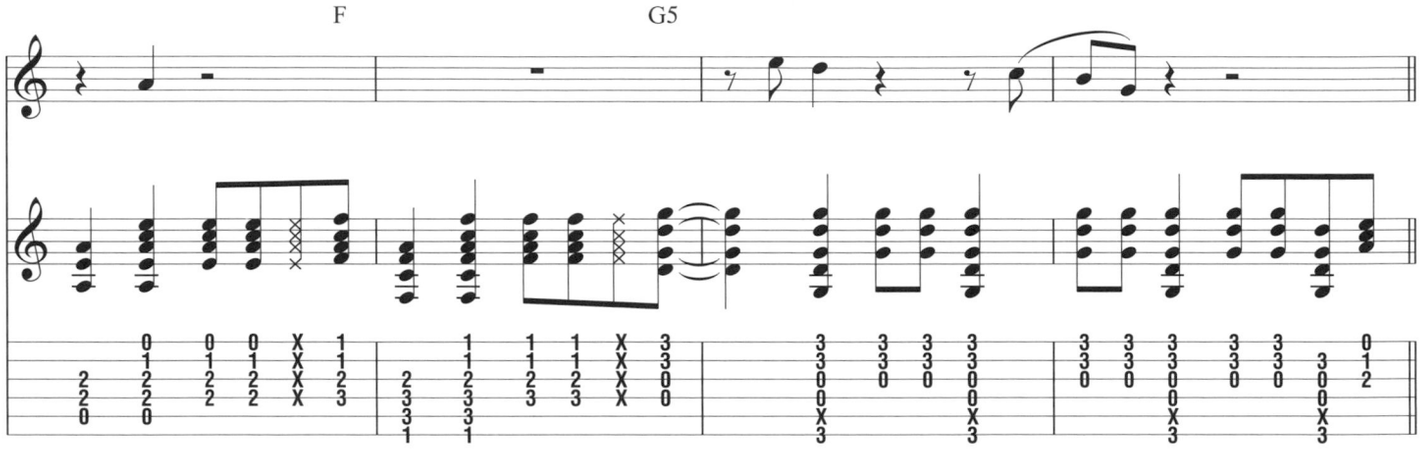
F
G5

Verse

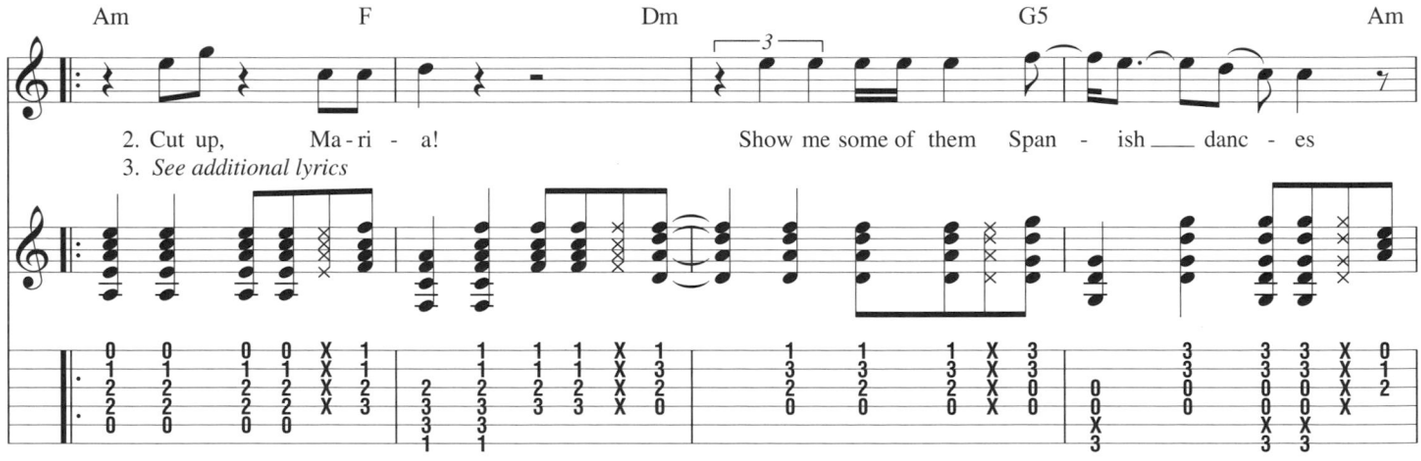
Am
F
Dm
G5
Am
2. Cut up, Ma - ri - a!
Show me some of them Span - ish danc - es
3. *See additional lyrics*

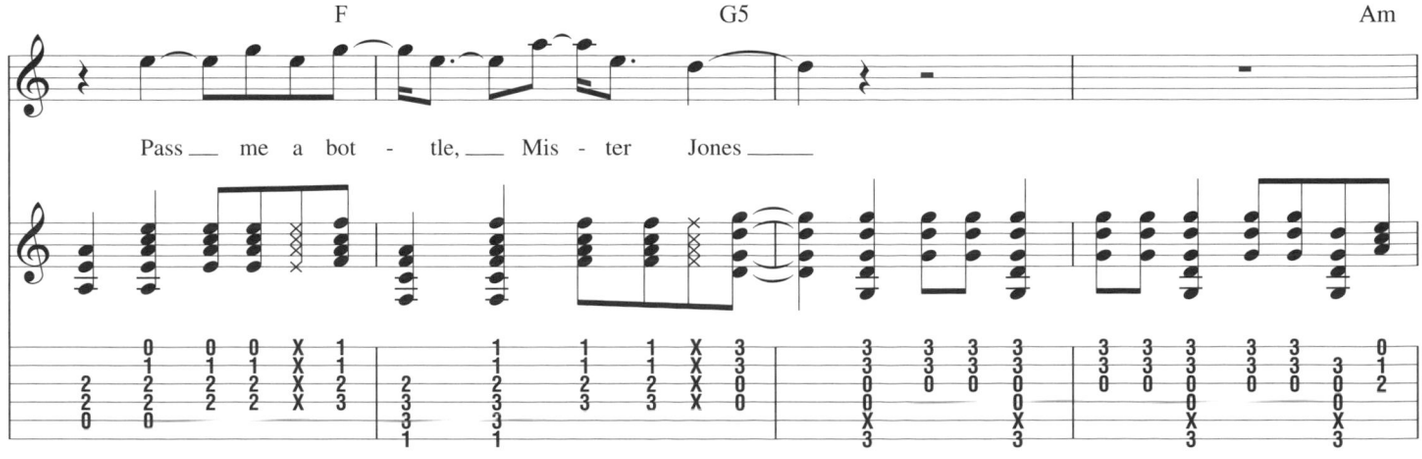
F
G5
Am
Pass me a bot - tle, Mis - ter Jones

F
Dm
G5
Am
Be - lieve in me
Help me be - lieve in an - y - thing
I

F
G5
C
want to be some - one who be - lieves

𝄋 **Chorus**

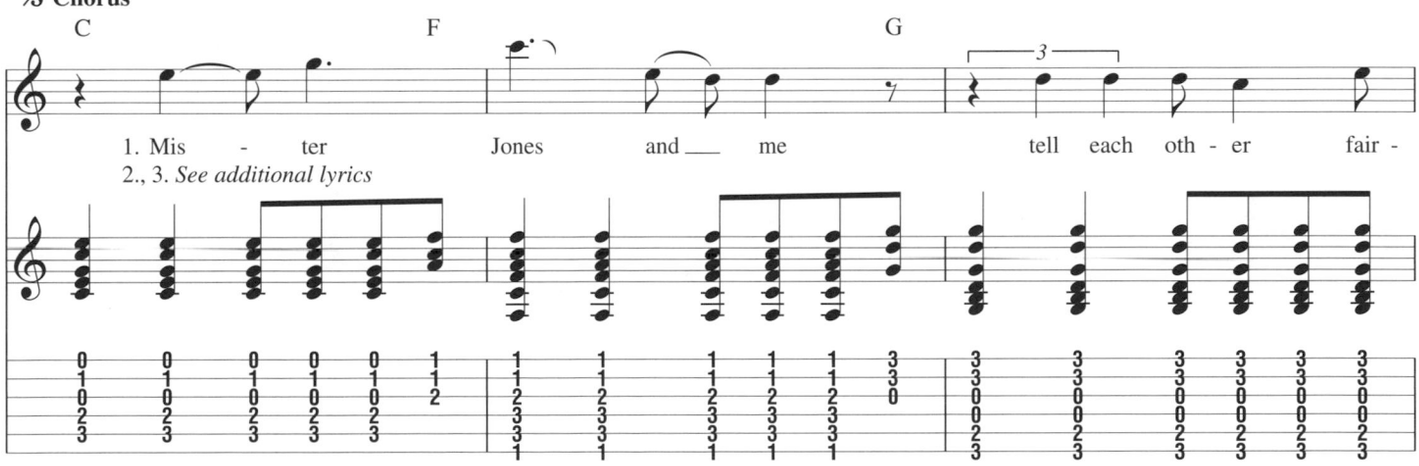
C
F
G
1. Mis - ter Jones and me tell each oth - er fair -
2., 3. *See additional lyrics*

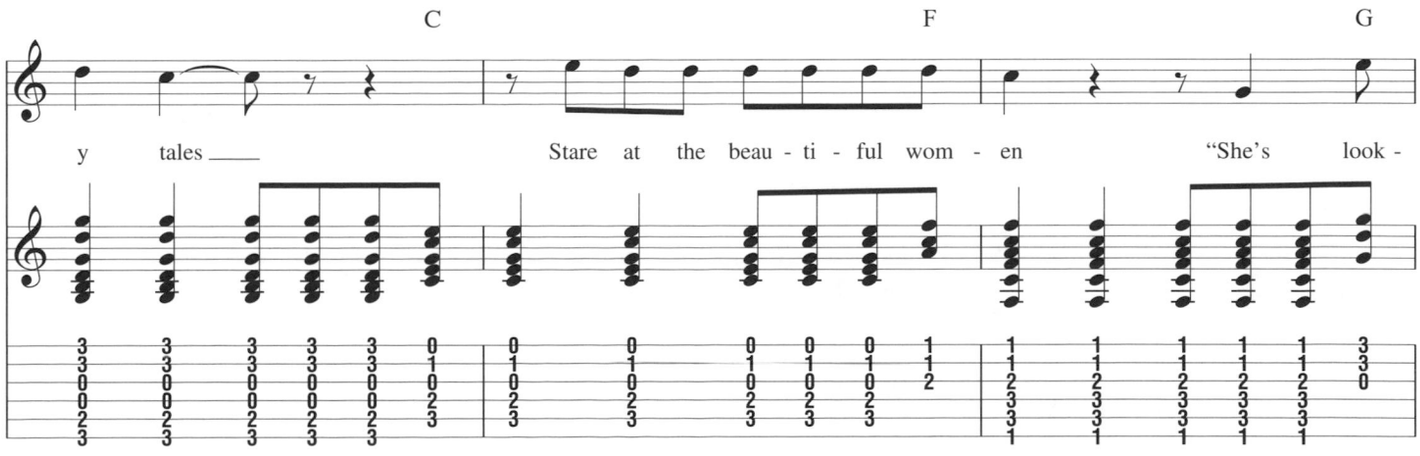
C
F
G
y tales
Stare at the beau - ti - ful wom - en
"She's look -

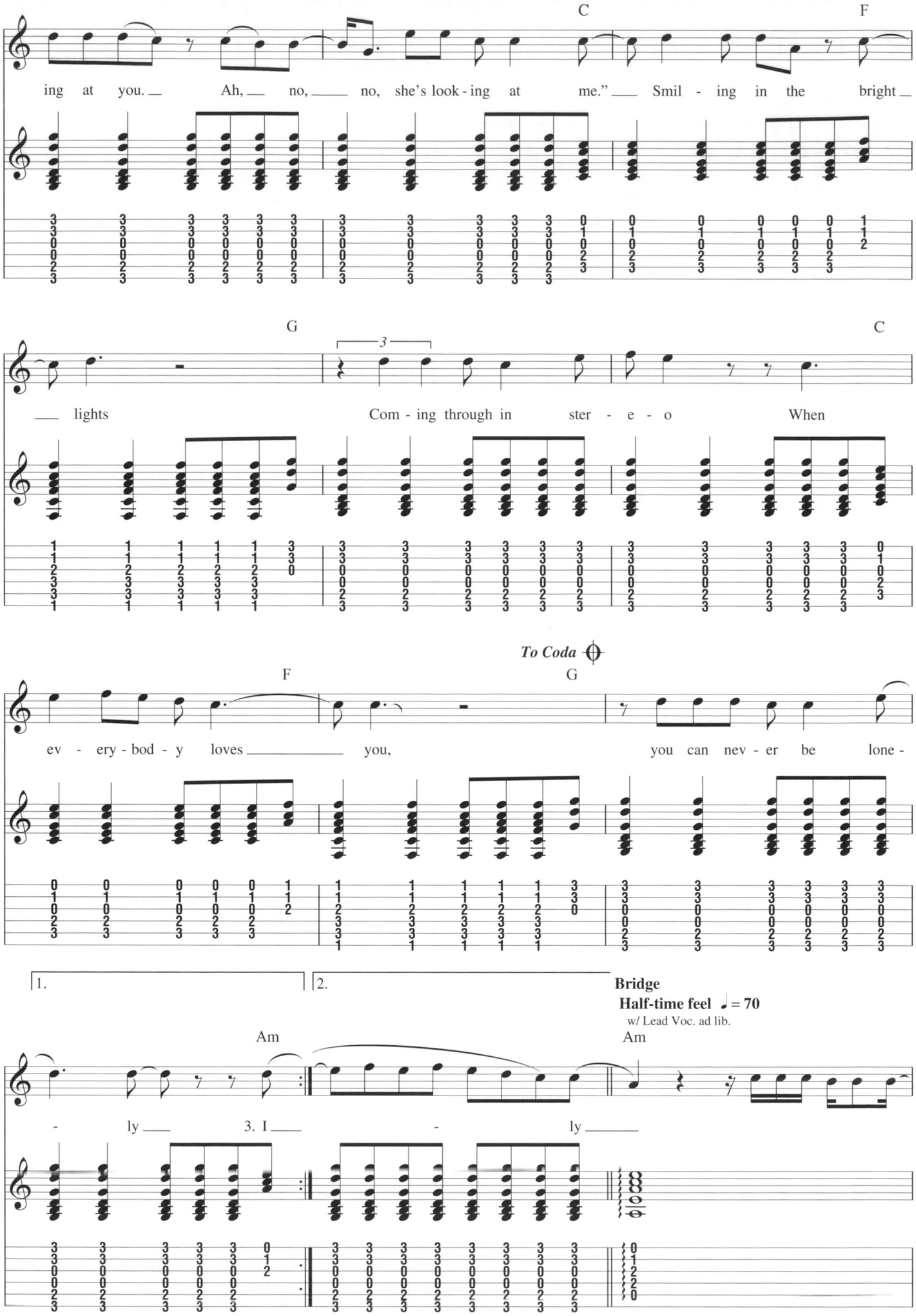
C
F
ing at you. Ah, no, no, she's look - ing at me." Smil - ing in the bright
G
C
3
lights
Com - ing through in ster - e - o
When
To Coda
F
G
ev - ery - bod - y loves you,
you can nev - er be lone -
1.
2.
Bridge
Half-time feel ♩ = 70
w/ Lead Voc. ad lib.
Am
Am
- ly 3. I - ly

Fmaj7
Am
G
*T
*T = Thumb on 6th stg.
Am
Fmaj7
I want to be a li - on
Ev - ery - bod - y wants to pass as cats
T
Am
G5
We all want to be big big stars, but we got dif - ferent rea - sons for that
Am
Fmaj7
Be - lieve in me Be-cause I don't be - lieve in an - y - thing and I
T

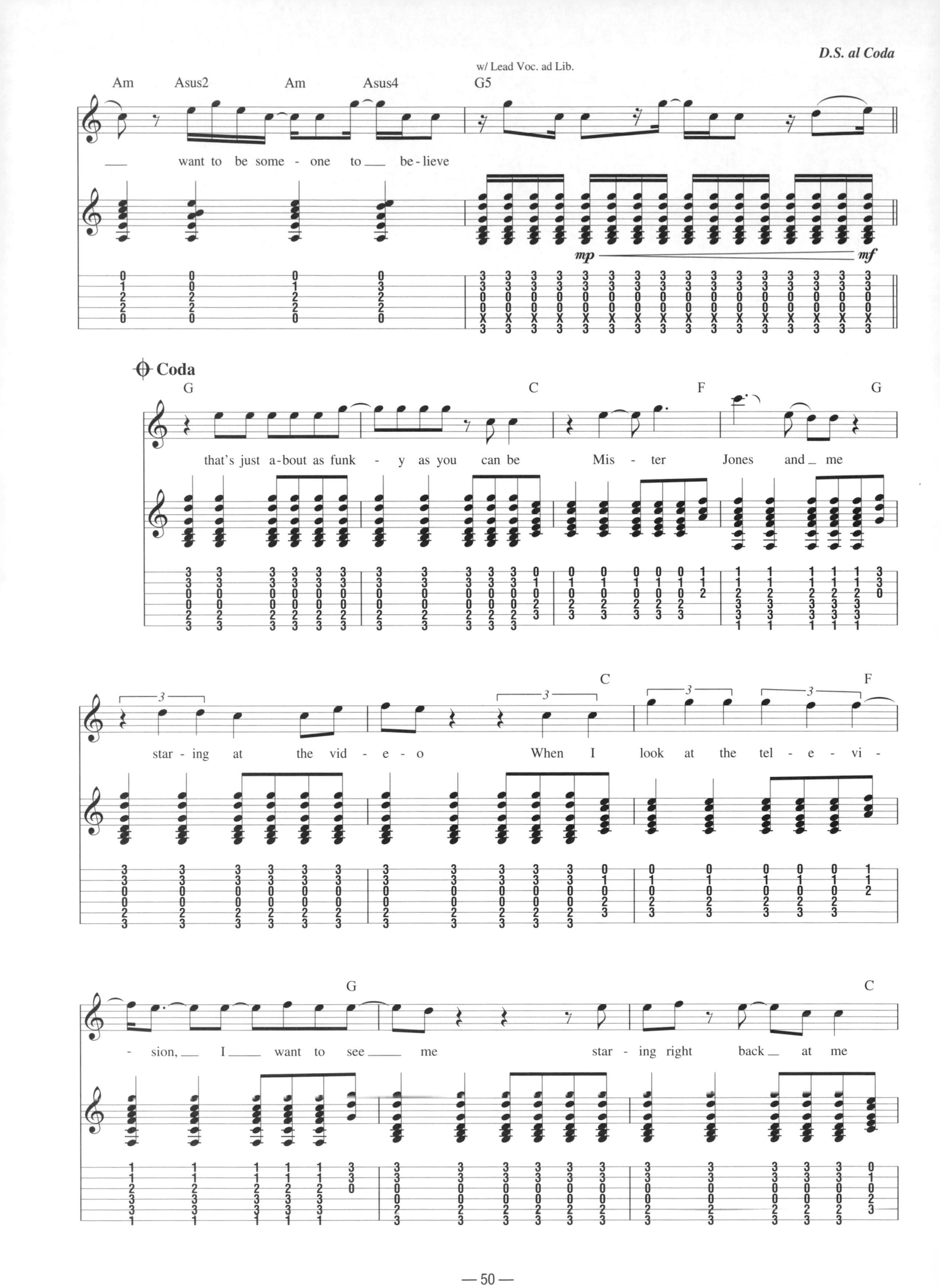
D.S. al Coda
w/ Lead Voc. ad Lib.
Am Asus2 Am Asus4 G5
want to be some - one to be - lieve
mp mf
Coda
G C F G
that's just a-bout as funk - y as you can be Mis - ter Jones and me
C F
star - ing at the vid - e - o When I look at the tel - e - vi -
G C
- sion, I want to see me star - ing right back at me

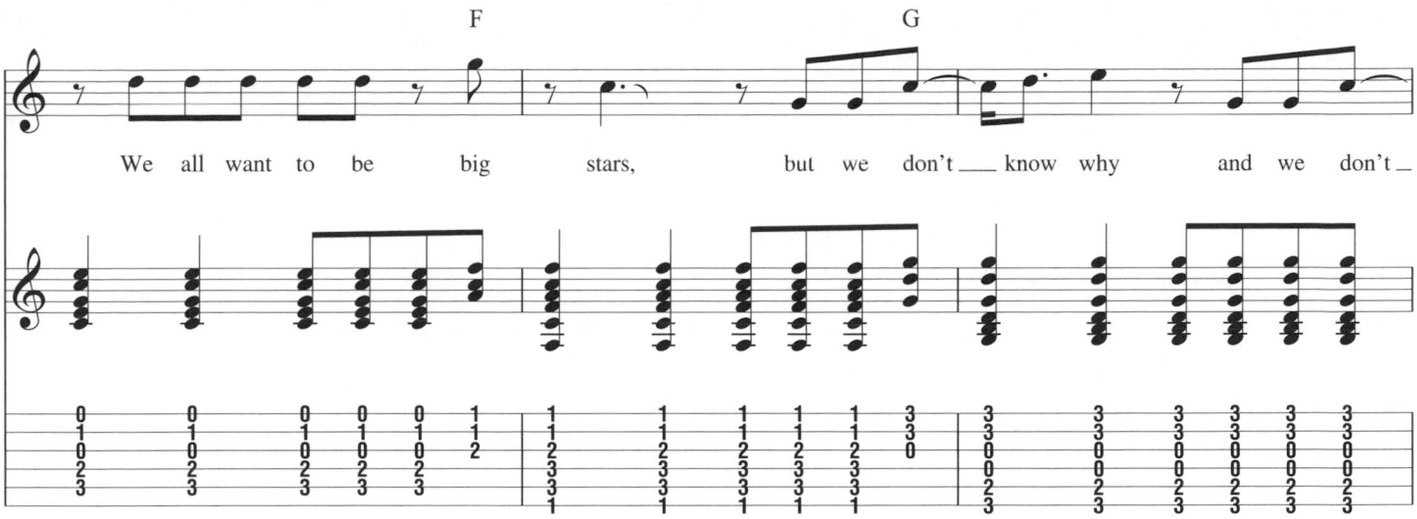
F
G
We all want to be big stars, but we don't know why and we don't

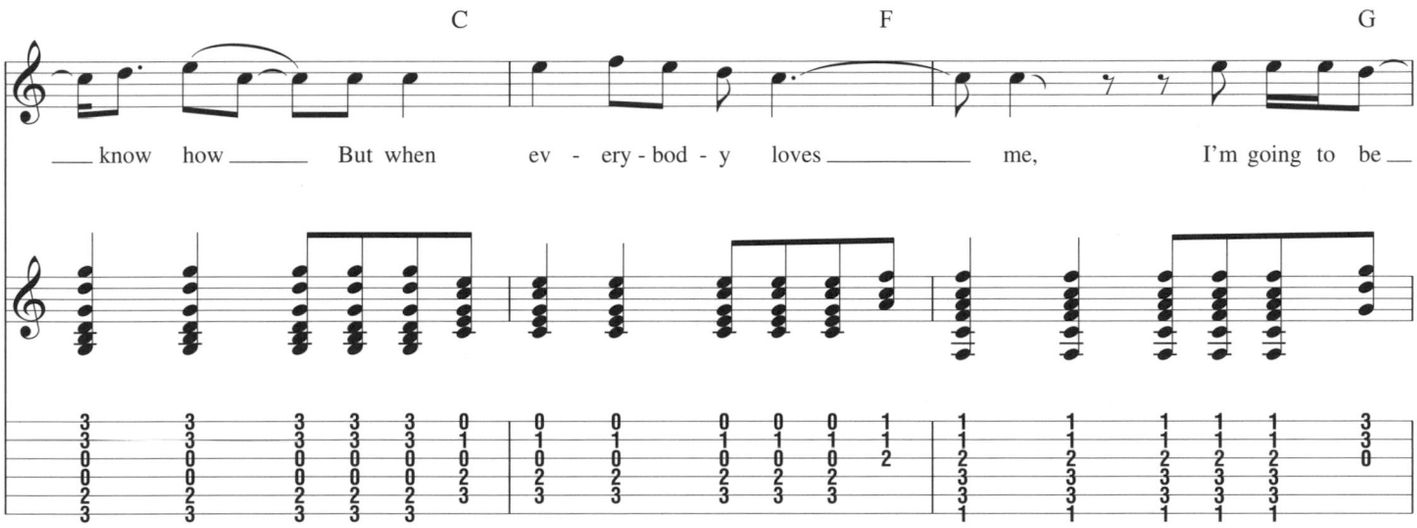
C
F
G
know how But when ev - ery - bod - y loves me, I'm going to be

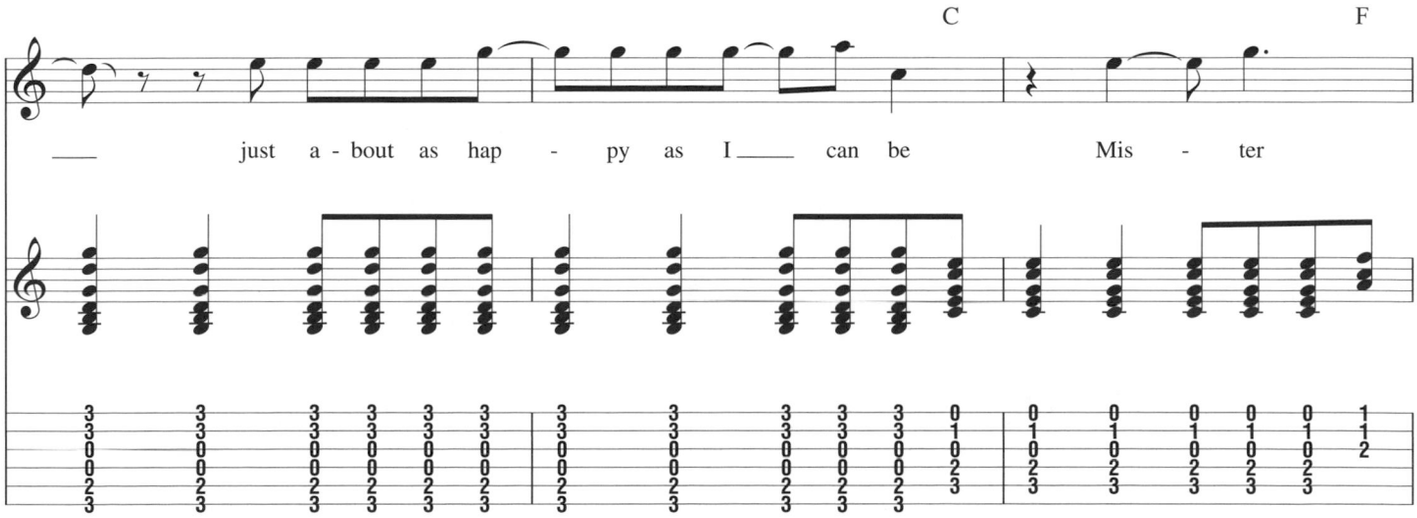
C
F
just a - bout as hap - py as I can be Mis - ter

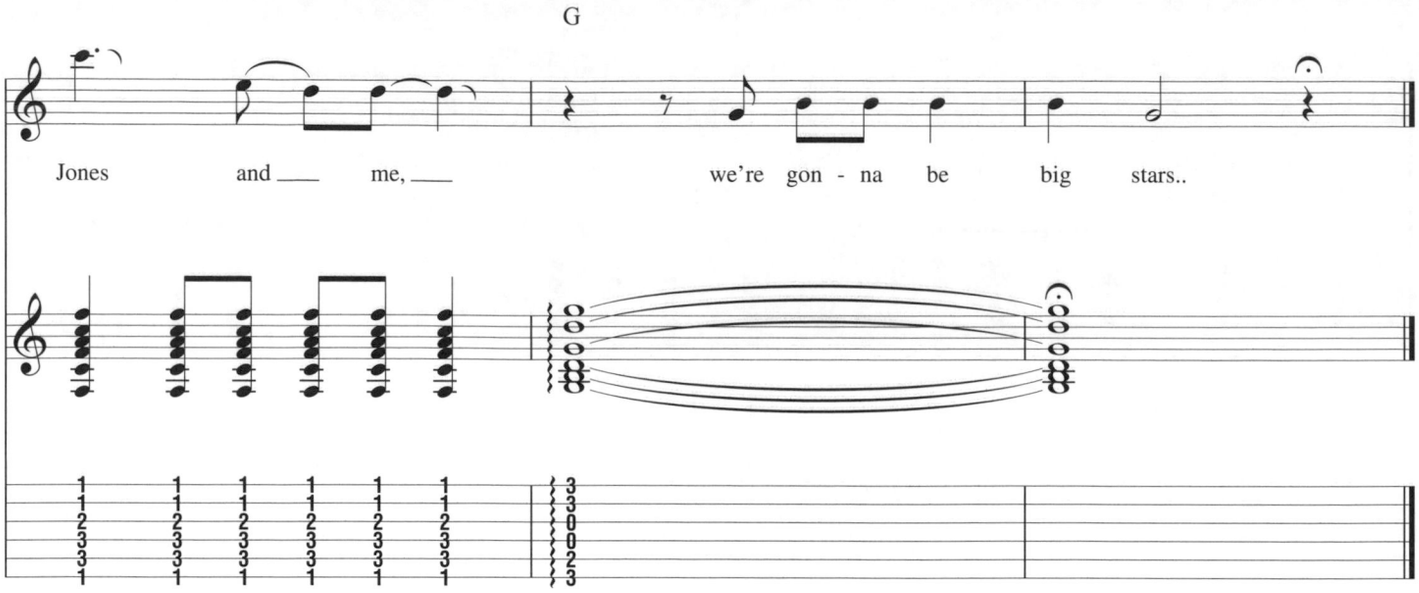

Additional Lyrics

3. I will paint my picture
Paint myself in blue and red and black and gray
All of the beautiful colors are very very meaningful
Gray is my favorite color
I felt so symbolic yesterday
If I knew Picaso I would buy myself a gray guitar and play

Chorus 2. Mr. Jones and me look into the future
Stare at the beautiful women
"She's looking at you.
Uh, I don't think so. She's looking at me."
Standing in the spotlight
I bought myself a gray guitar
When everybody loves me, I will never be lonely

Chorus 3. Mr. Jones and me stumbling through the barrio
Yeah we stare at the beautiful women
"She's perfect for you, Man, there's got to be
somebody for me."
I wanna be Bob Dylan
Mr. Jones wishes he was someone just a little more
funky
When everybody loves you, son, that's just about as
funky as you can be

MORE THAN WORDS
Extreme

Video Lesson – 22 minutes, 30 seconds

Tune Down 1/2 Step: (low to high) E♭–A♭–D♭–G♭–B♭–E♭
Key of G

Guitar Tone:

- steel-string or nylon-string acoustic guitar
- medium reverb

Chords:

Intro:

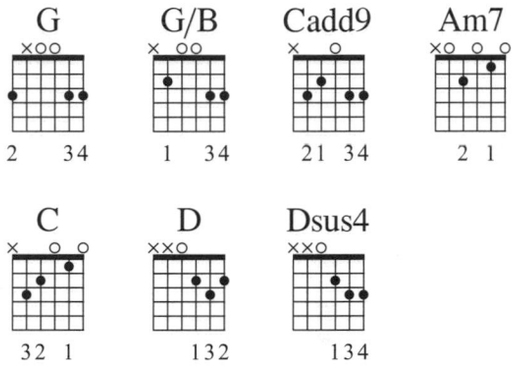

Verse:

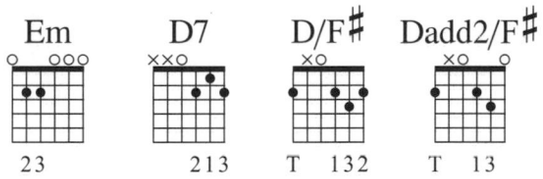

Chorus:

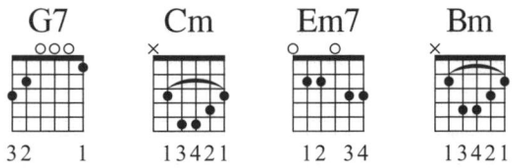

Techniques:

- Pick-Hand Slap: throughout almost the entire song, the pick hand slaps the strings on beats 2 and 4. Instead of slapping with an open hand, come down in position ready to pluck the next chord.
- Fingerstyle: put your pick away for this one, it's played exclusively with the fingers! If this is a new technique for you, keep the fingers lightly arched and pluck the strings with the fingers moving towards the palm, in a piano (or block) style of picking.
- Guitar Body Slap: slap the body of the guitar with your pick hand, either behind the bridge or on the upper bout.
- Thumb-Fretting: for the D/F♯ and Dadd2/F♯, fret the F♯ on the 6th string with the side of your fret-hand thumb. You may have to adjust your normal fret-hand position to make this comfortable.
- Two-Handed Tapping: the free time ending features some two-handed tapping. Use either the index or middle finger of the pick hand to tap the notes at the indicated frets.
- Neck Bend: this is not a recommended technique! But if you want to try and emulate the sound on the original recording, gently grab your headstock with your fret hand while creating opposing pressure with your pick hand just above where the neck joins the body. Lightly push in opposite directions. The key term is *lightly*!

More Than Words

Words and Music by Nuno Bettencourt and Gary Cherone

Tune down 1/2 step:
(low to high) E♭-A♭-D♭-G♭-B♭-E♭

Intro

Moderately slow ♩ = 96

G G/B Cadd9 Am7 C D Dsus4 G

mf

w/ fingers

let ring throughout

*Slap muted strings w/ R.H. throughout.

G/B Cadd9 Am7 C D Dsus4 G

Verse

G G/B Cadd9 Am7 C

1. Say - ing "I love you" is not the words I want

Copyright © 1990 COLOR ME BLIND MUSIC
All Rights Administered by ALMO MUSIC CORP.
All Rights Reserved Used by Permission

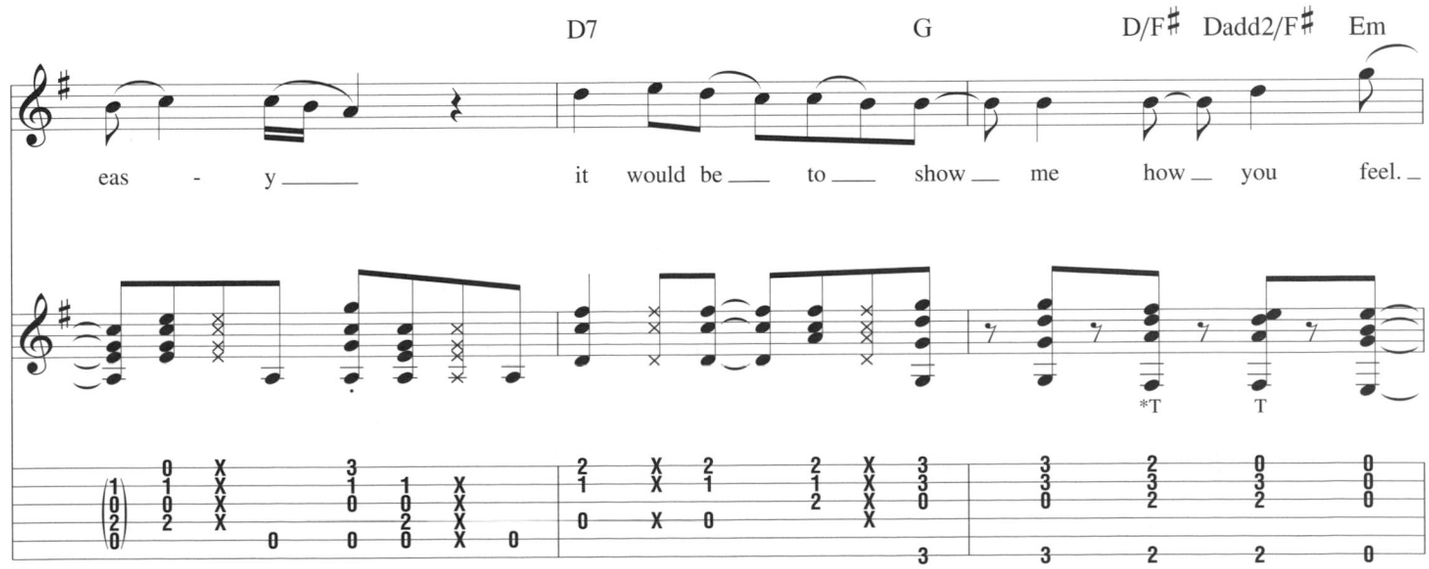

*T = Thumb on 6th string

Chorus
Am7
D7
G7
More than words is all you have to do
G7/B
C
Cm
G
to make it real. Then you would - n't have to say
Em7
Am7
D7
that you love me, 'cause I'd al - read - y

G
Dadd2/F♯
Em
know. What would you do ___ if my heart _

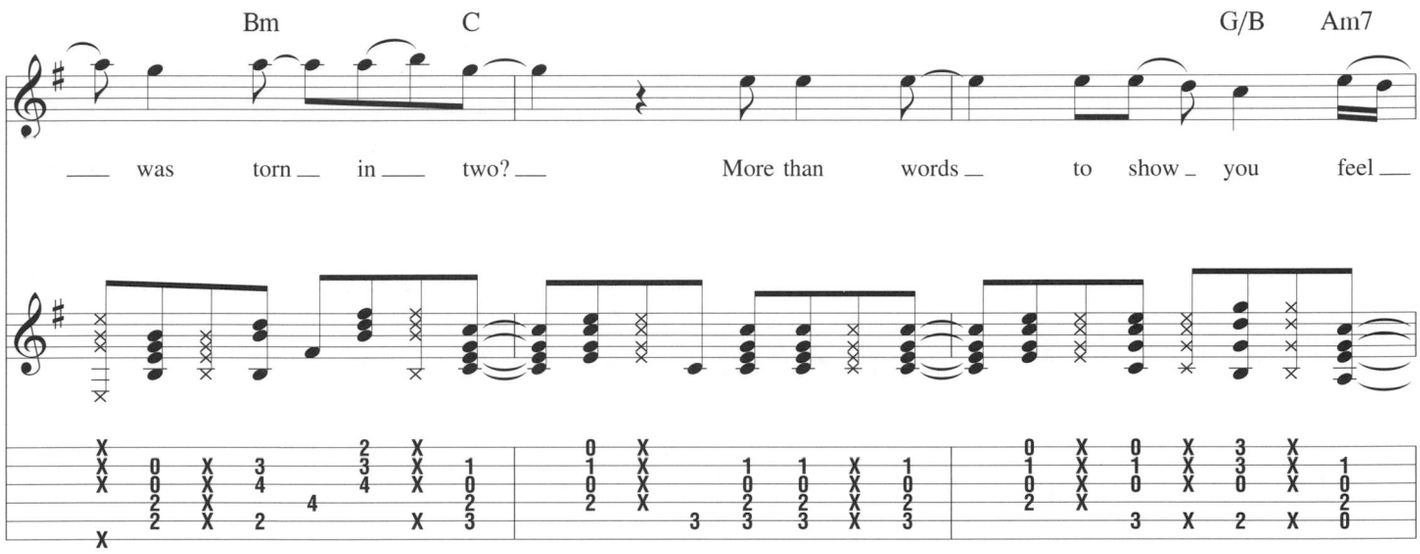
Bm
C
G/B
Am7
___ was torn _ in ___ two? ___ More than words _ to show _ you feel ___

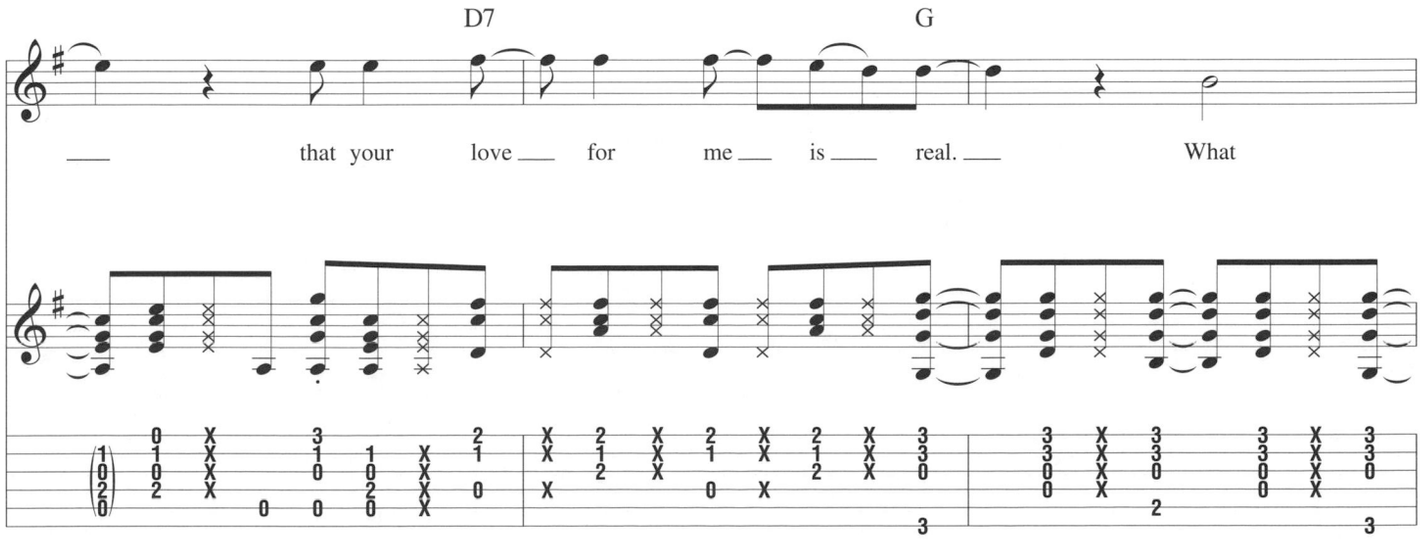
D7
G
___ that your love ___ for me ___ is ___ real. ___ What

Dadd2/F♯
Em
Bm
C
would you say if I took those words a - way?
G/B
Am7
Then you could - n't make things new just by say -
Interlude
D7
G
G/B
Cadd9
Am7
- ing "I love you."
(You.
La, dee, da, la, dee, da,
La, dee, da.)

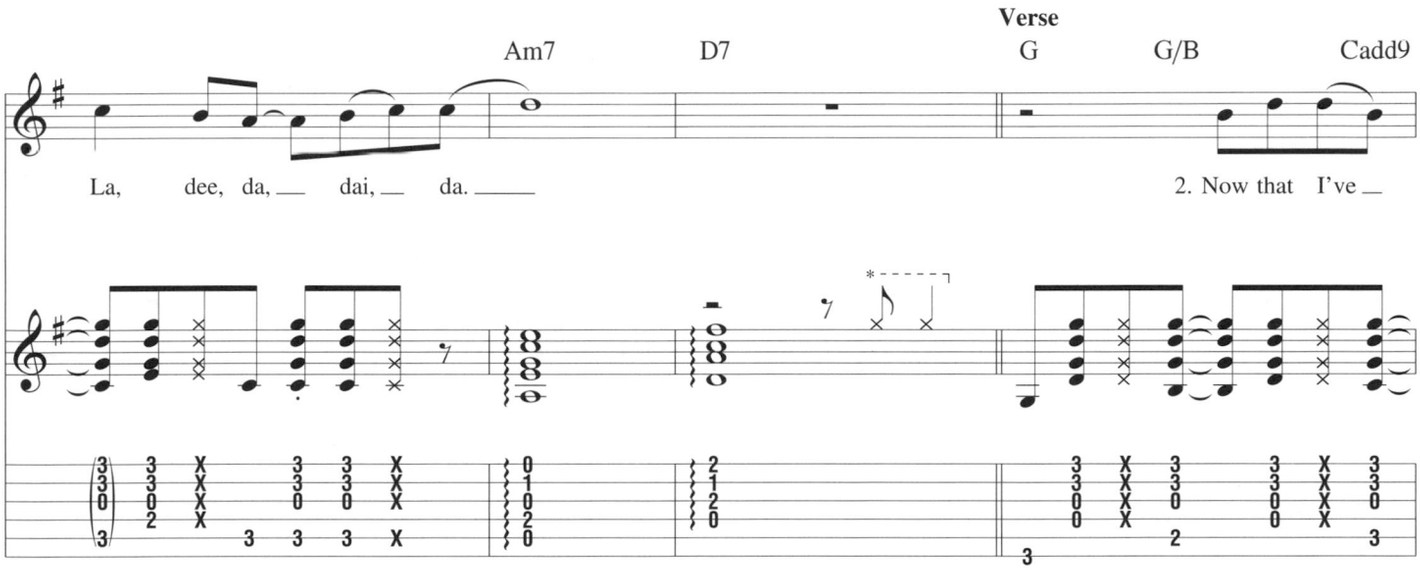

*Slap body of gtr.

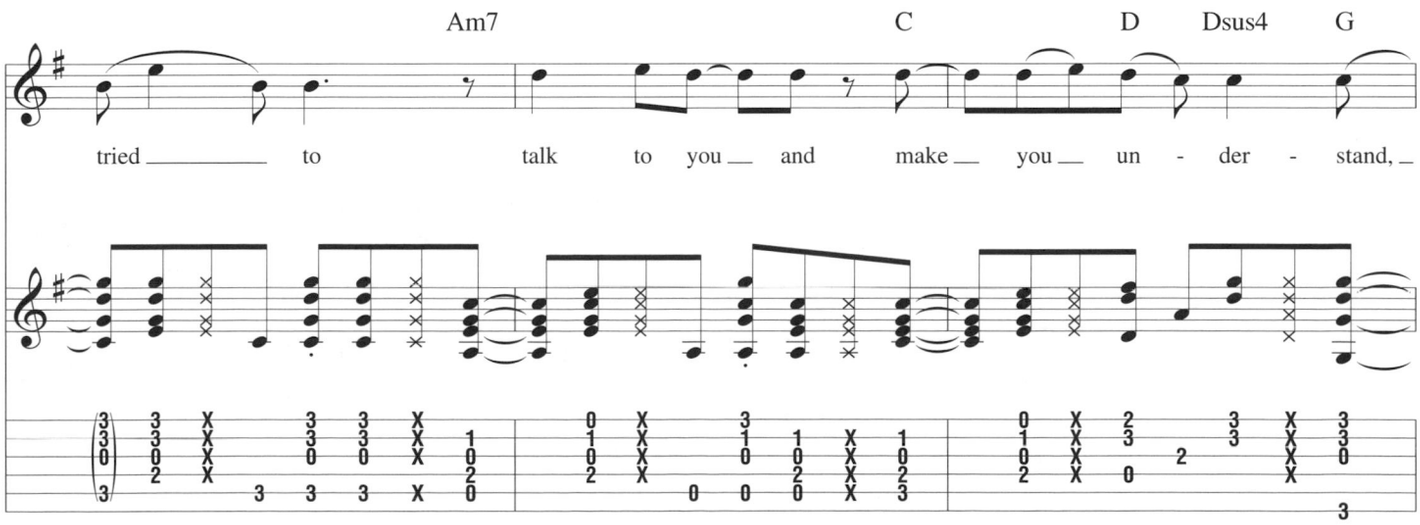

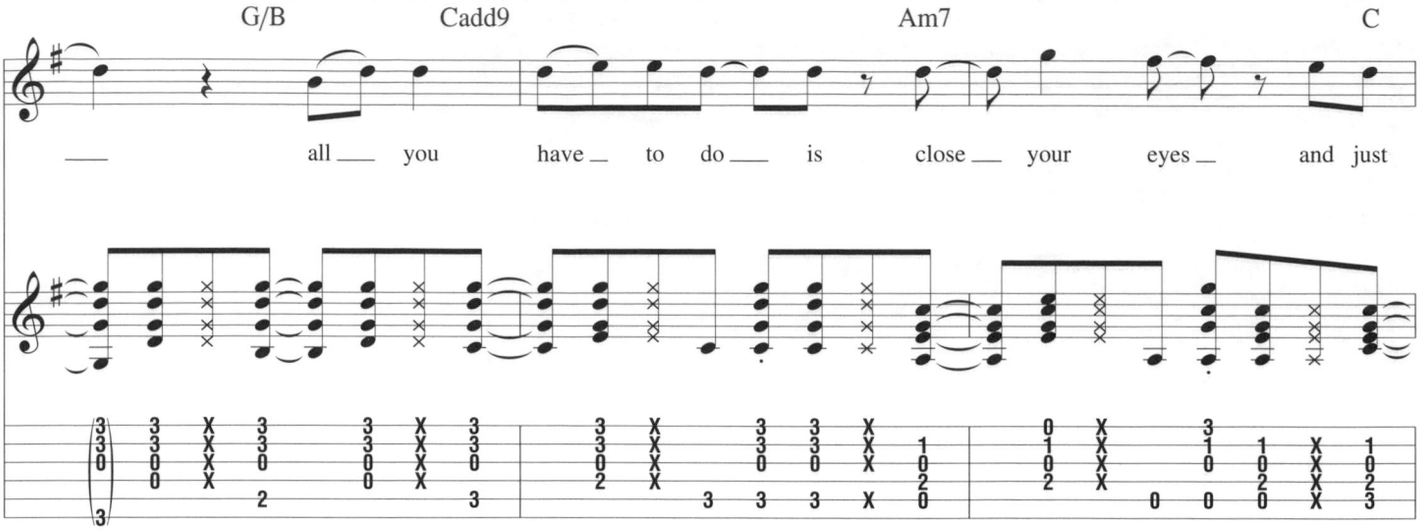

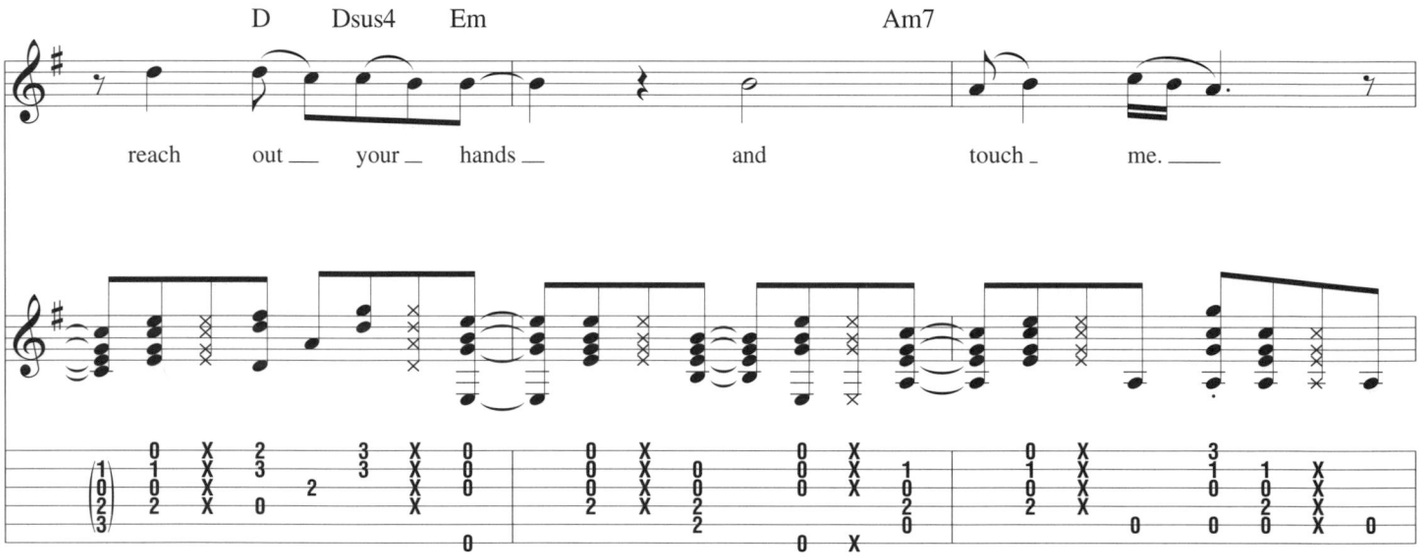

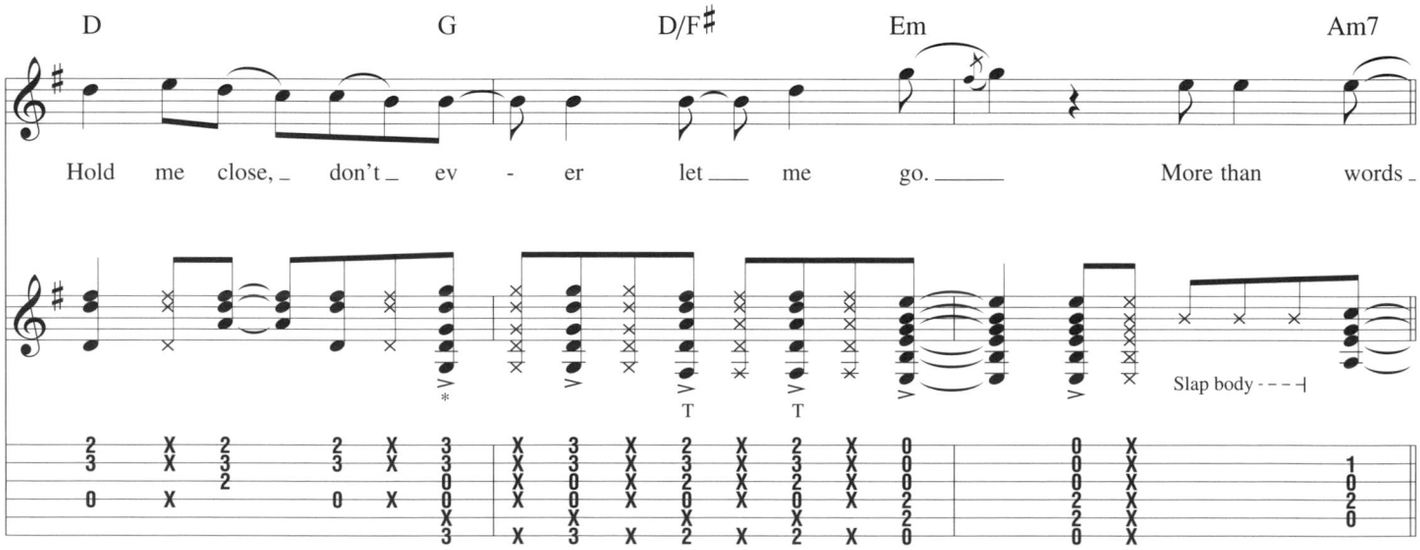

*Strum accented chords w/ nails (all downstrokes);
hit muted strings w/ R.H. as before.

Chorus
Am7
D7
G7
G7/B
C
is all I ev - er need - ed you to show.
Cm
G
Em7
Then you would - n't have to say that you love
Am7
D
D7♭9/A
G
me, 'cause I'd al - read - y know.
What

Dadd2/F♯
Em
Bm
C
would you do if my heart was torn in two?

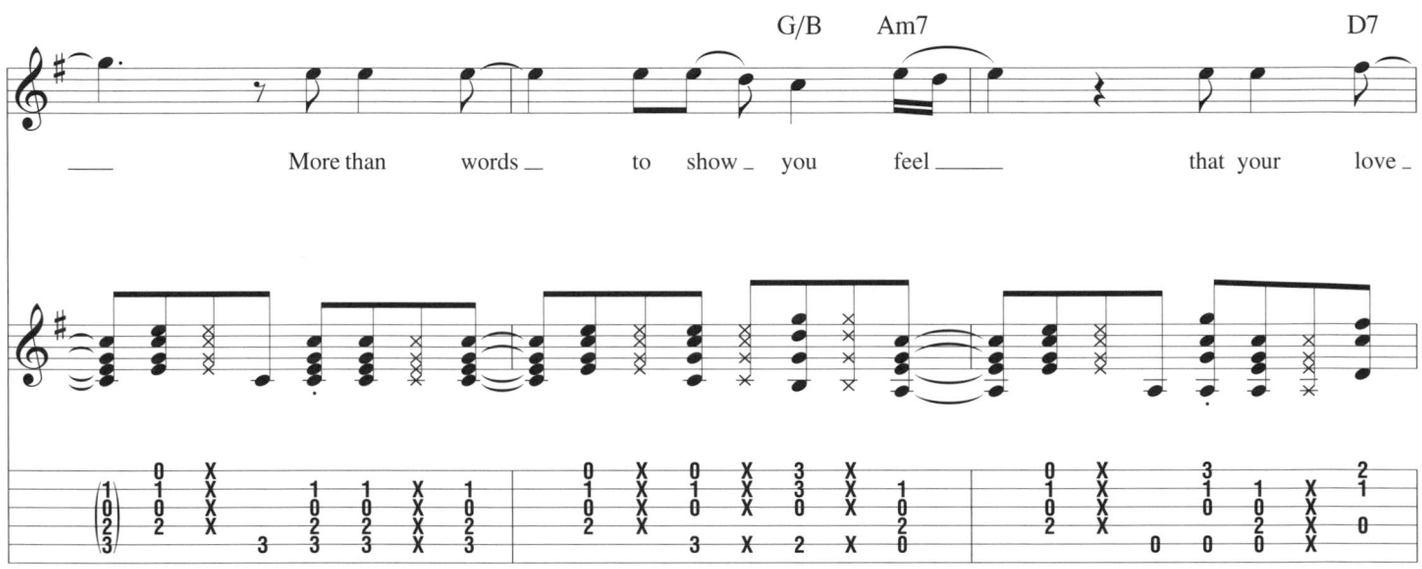
G/B
Am7
D7
More than words to show you feel that your love

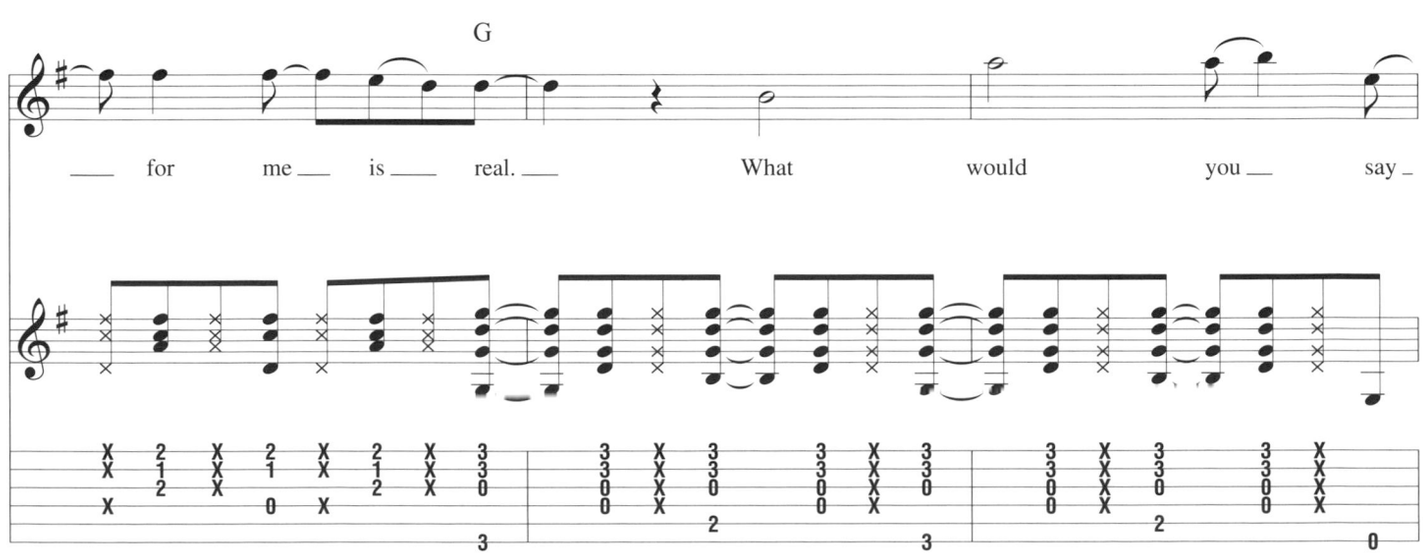
G
for me is real. What would you say

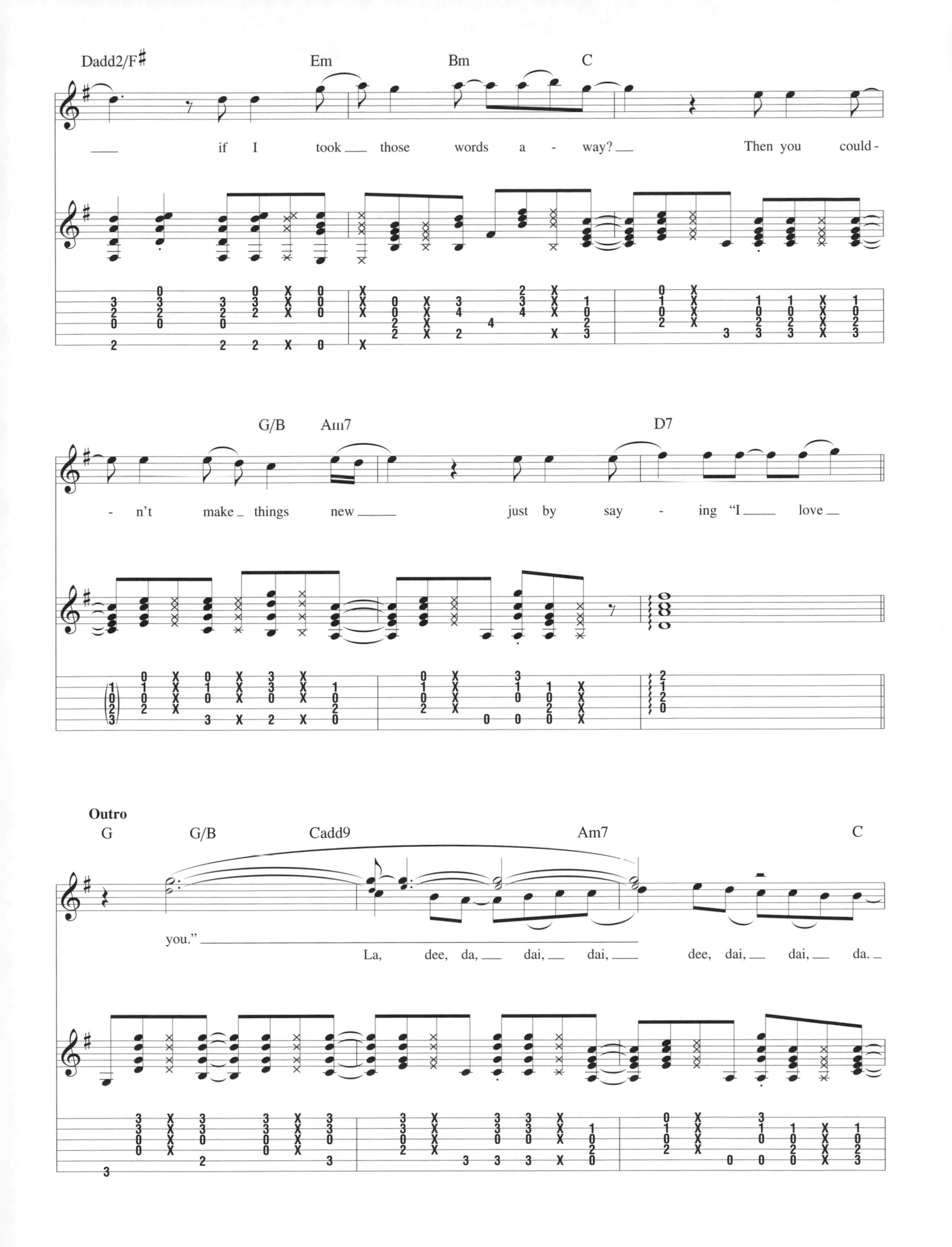
Dadd2/F♯
Em
Bm
C
if I took those words a - way? Then you could -
G/B
Am7
D7
- n't make things new just by say - ing "I love
Outro
G
G/B
Cadd9
Am7
C
you."
La, dee, da, dai, dai, dee, dai, dai, da.

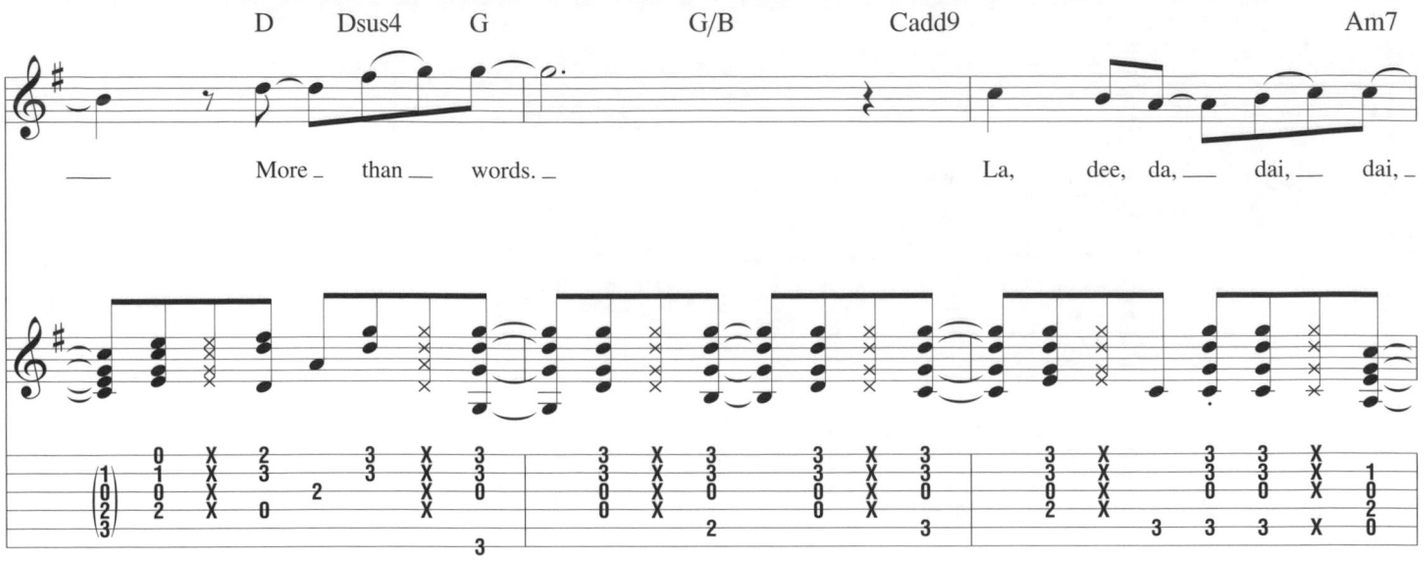
D Dsus4 G G/B Cadd9 Am7
More than words.
La, dee, da, dai, dai,

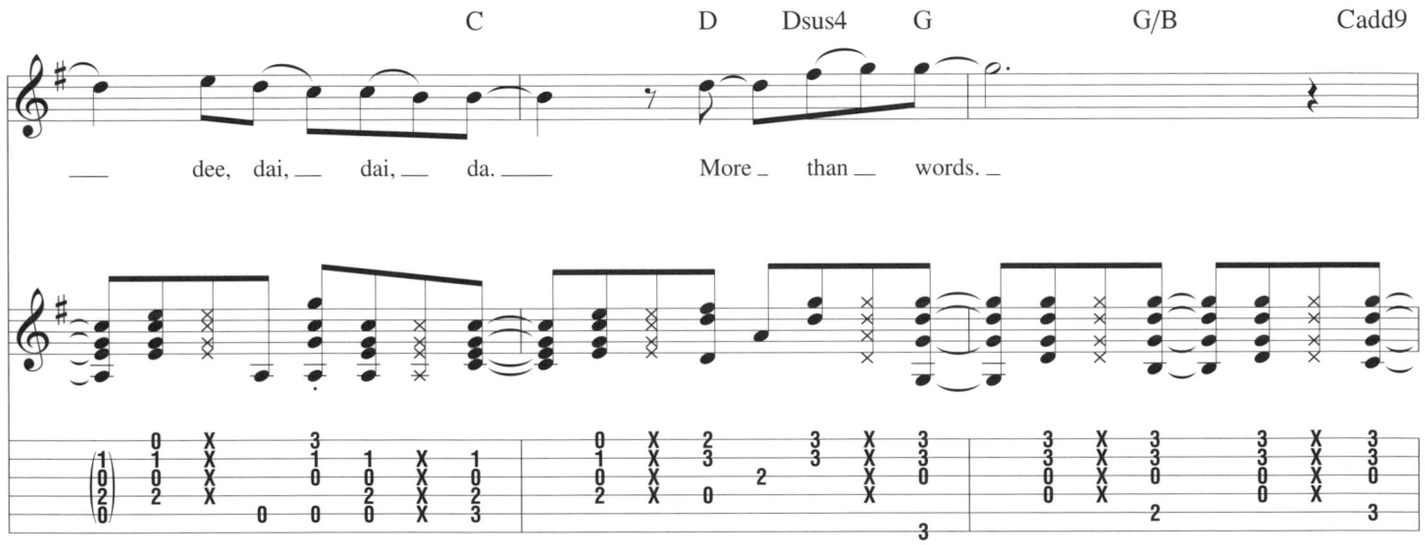
C D Dsus4 G G/B Cadd9
dee, dai, dai, da.
More than words.

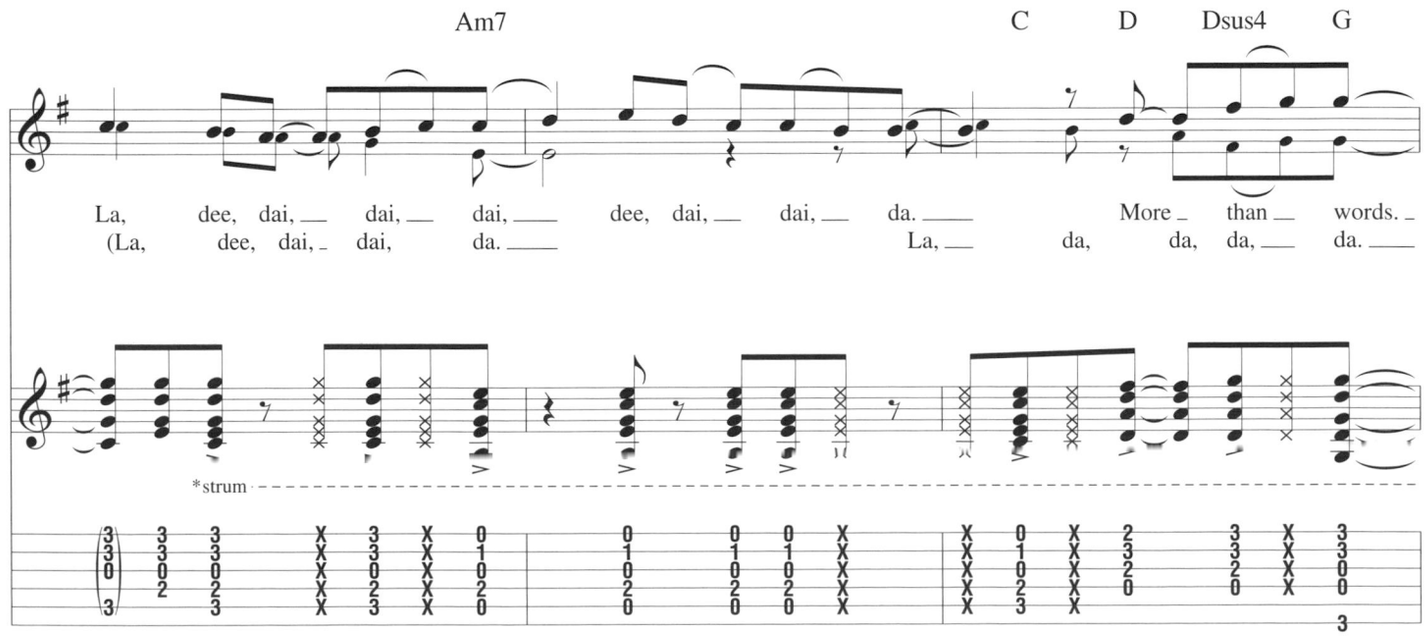
Am7 C D Dsus4 G
La, dee, dai, dai, dai, dee, dai, dai, da.
More than words.
(La, dee, dai, dai, da.
La, da, da, da, da.
*strum
*As before

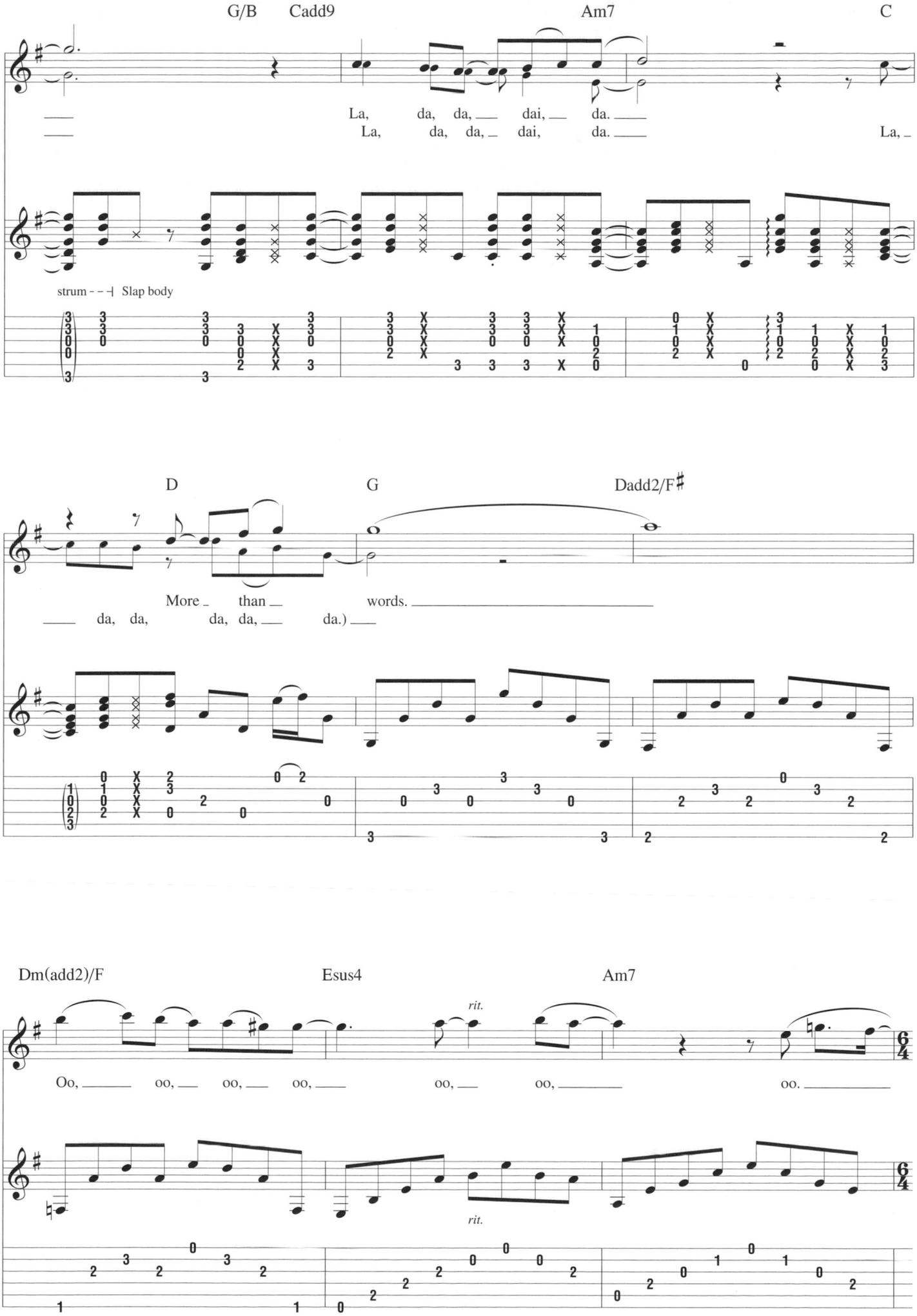
G/B
Cadd9
Am7
C
La, da, da, dai, da.
La, da, da, dai, da.
La,
strum - - - Slap body
D
G
Dadd2/F♯
More than words.
da, da, da, da, da.)
Dm(add2)/F
Esus4
Am7
rit.
Oo, oo, oo, oo, oo, oo, oo.
rit.

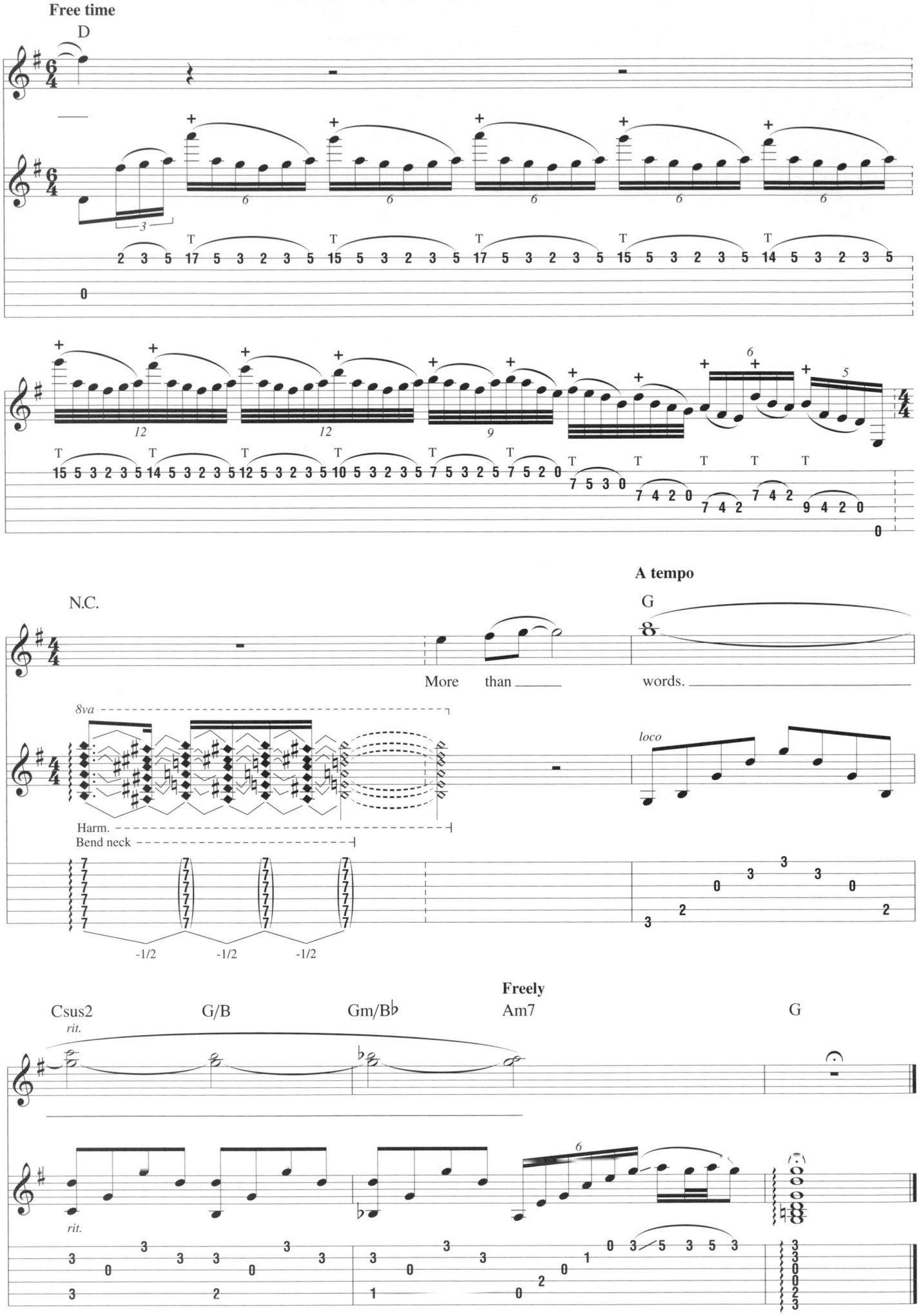
Free time
D
N.C.
More than
words.
A tempo
G
8va
loco
Harm.
Bend neck
-1/2
-1/2
-1/2
Csus2
rit.
G/B
Gm/B♭
Freely
Am7
G
rit.

PATIENCE
Guns N' Roses

Video Lesson – 23 minutes, 13 seconds

Tune Down 1/2 Step: (low to high) E♭–A♭–D♭–G♭–B♭–E♭
Key of G, D

Guitar Tone:

- steel-string acoustic guitar

Chords:

Intro/Verse/Chorus:

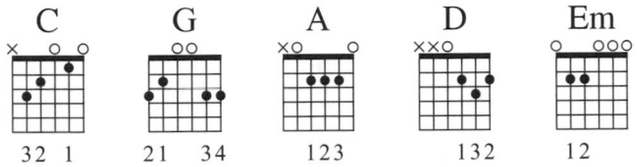

Outro:

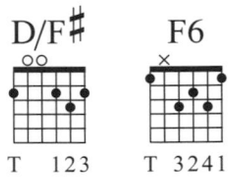

Scales:

Guitar Solos:

G Major Scale

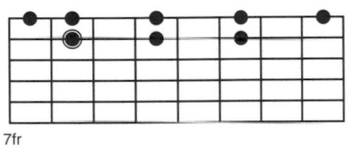

Techniques:

- Strumming: it's not necessary to strum all the notes of each chord every time. Strive for a loose strumming feel, striking only some of the strings within each chord. This will sound more natural and musical. Generally, downstrokes tend to catch the lower three strings and upstrokes catch the higher three strings.
- Thumb-Fretting: for the D/F♯ and F6 chords in the Outro, wrap your fret-hand thumb over the neck to fret the bass notes on the 6th string. If you're not comfortable using your thumb, you can use your 1st finger instead, but it makes the chords more difficult to fret.
- Dyads: for the 6th intervals in the opening Guitar Solo, fret the notes on the 3rd string with the middle finger and the notes on the 1st string with the ring or index (depending on the shape). Your middle finger should be lightly touching the 2nd string to mute it. Then you can strum through the top three strings for each dyad and only two strings will produce sound.
- String Bending: on an acoustic guitar, bends are usually more difficult because of the higher tension and thicker strings. Be sure to use support fingers behind the bending finger to add some strength. You can also try lighter gauge strings. Another alternative is to replace the bends with slides if you just can't get those strings bent up to pitch.

Patience

Words and Music by W. Axl Rose, Slash, Izzy Stradlin', Duff McKagan and Steven Adler

Tune down 1/2 step:
(low to high) E♭-A♭-D♭-G♭-B♭-E♭

Intro
Moderate Rock ♩ = 120
Half-time feel

Copyright © 1988 Guns N' Roses Music (ASCAP) and Black Frog Music (ASCAP)
All Rights for Black Frog Music in the U.S. and Canada Controlled and Administered by Universal - PolyGram International Publishing, Inc.
International Copyright Secured All Rights Reserved

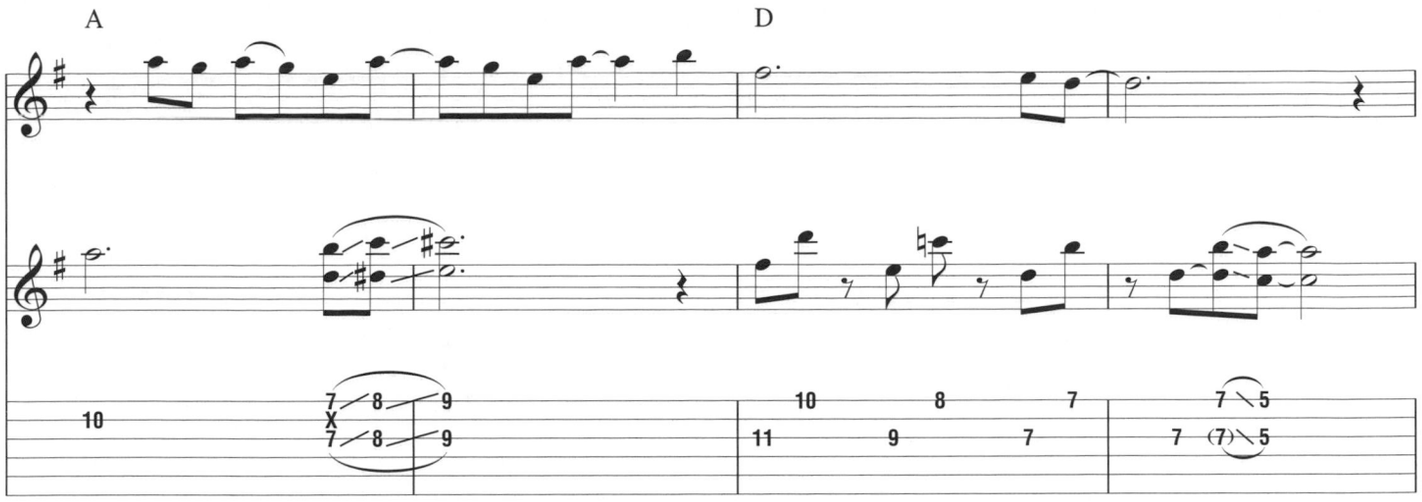
A
D

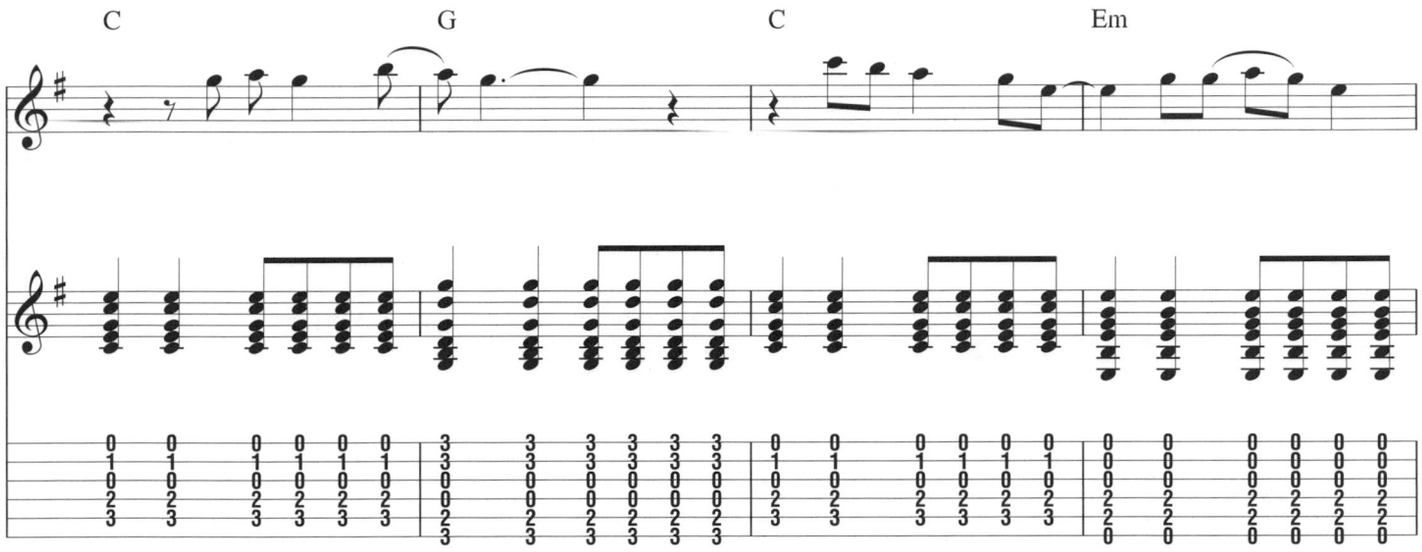
C
G
C
Em

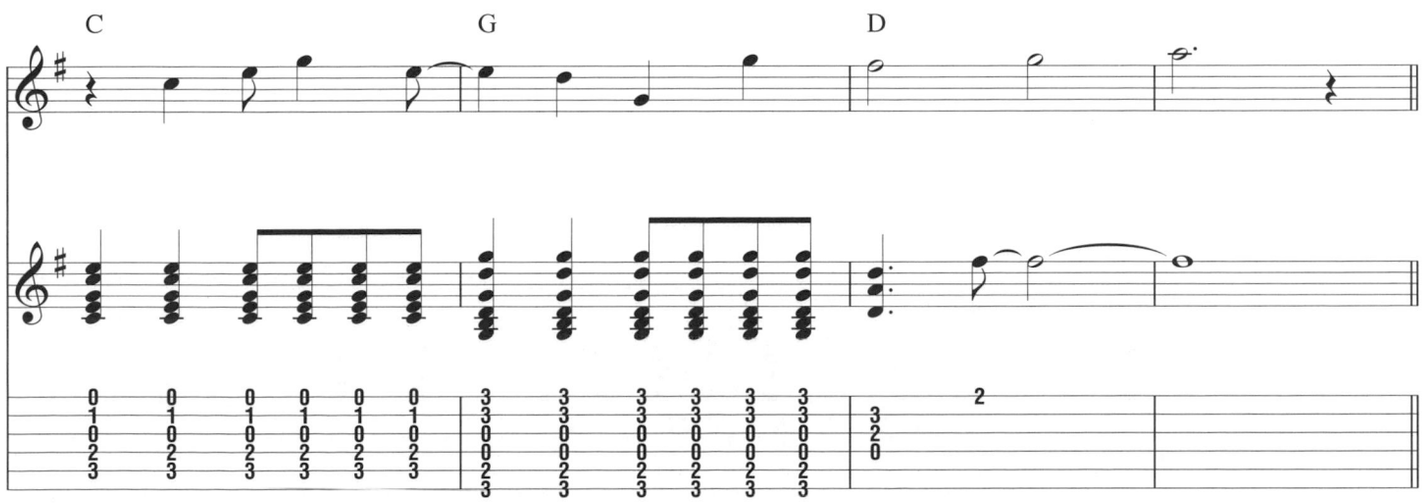
C
G
D

Verse
C
G
1. Shed a tear 'cause I'm miss - in' you,
I'm still al - right to smile.
2. See additional lyrics

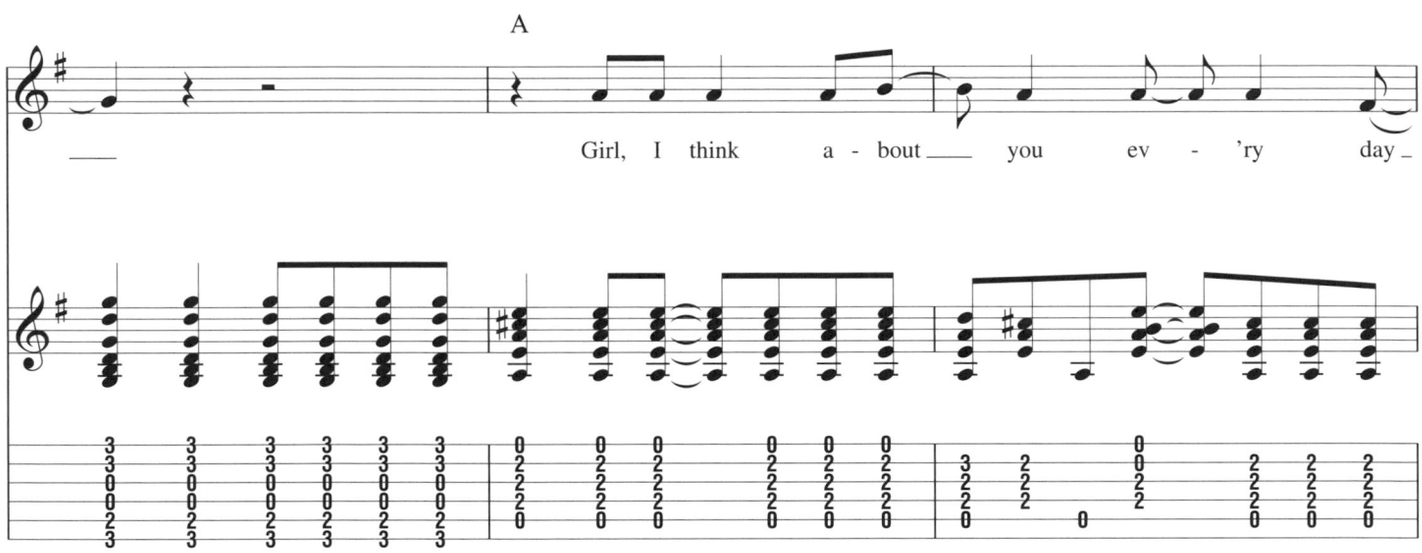
A
Girl, I think a - bout you ev - 'ry day

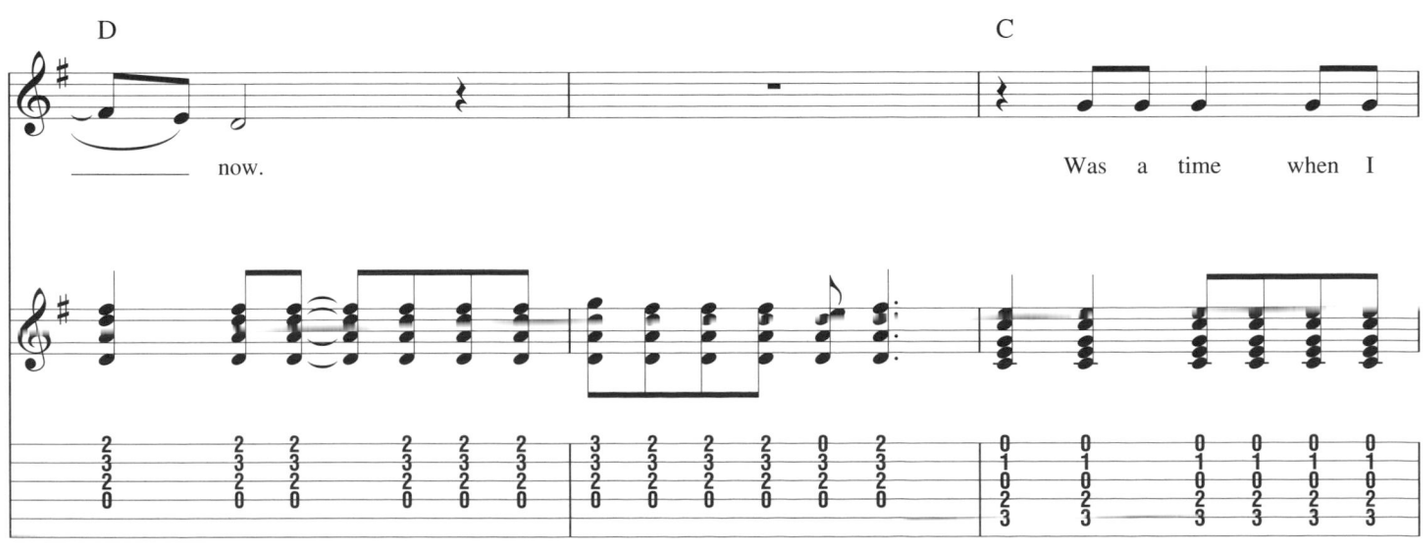
D
now.
C
Was a time when I

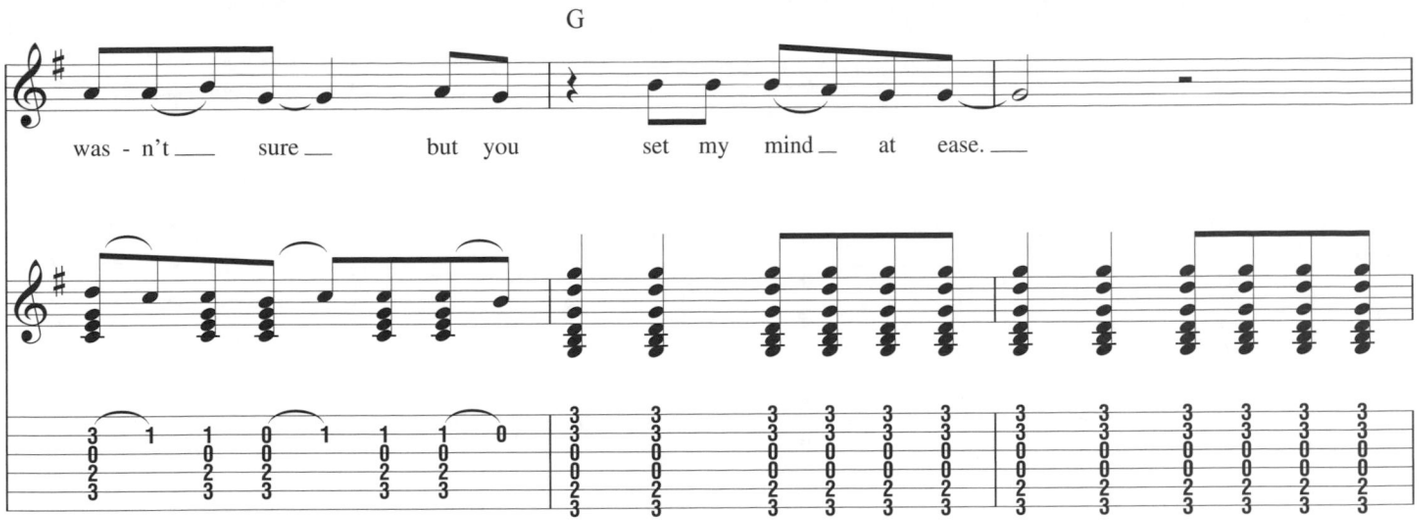

Chorus

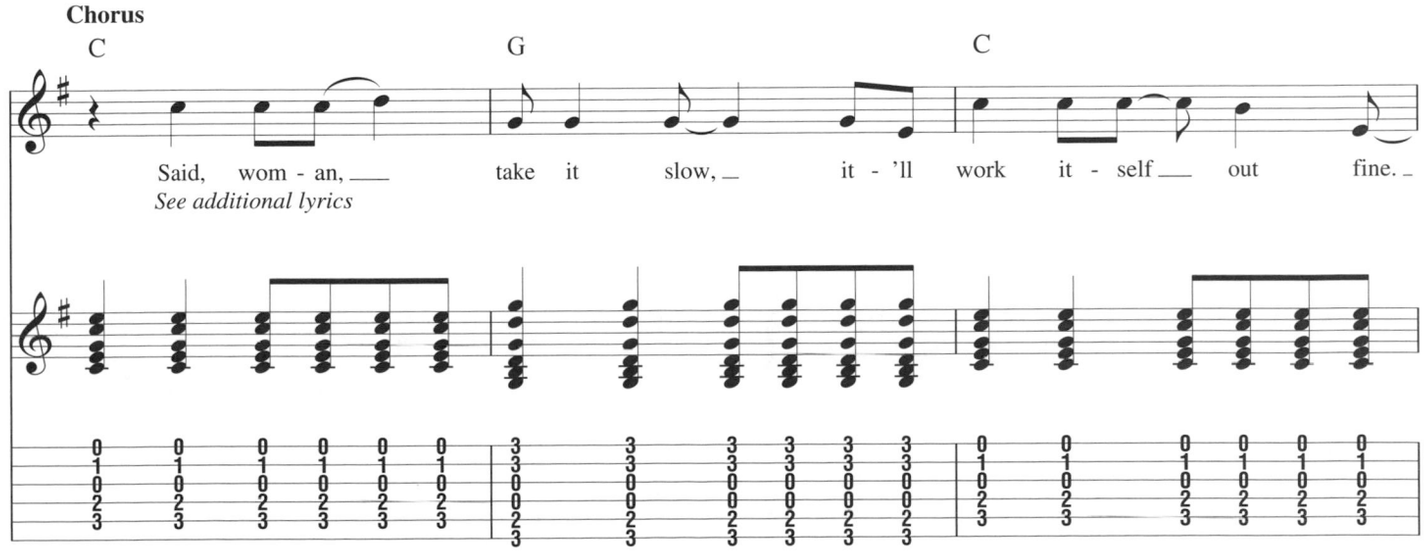

See additional lyrics

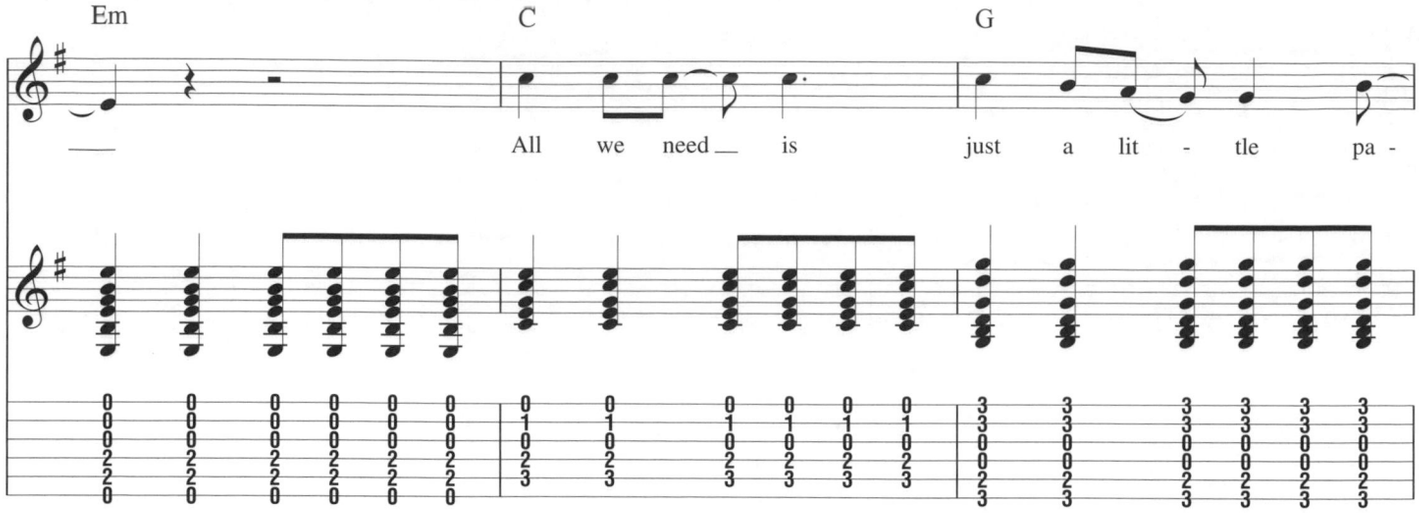
Em
C
G
All we need is just a lit - tle pa -

D
C
- tience.
Said, Sug - ar,

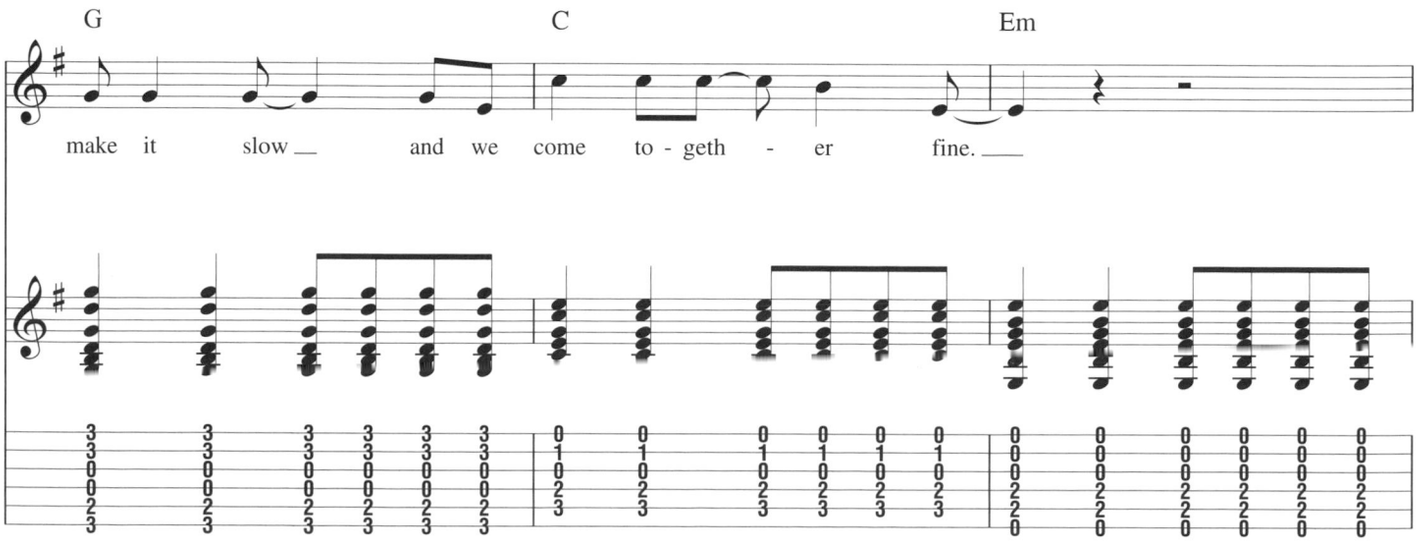
G
C
Em
make it slow and we come to - geth - er fine.

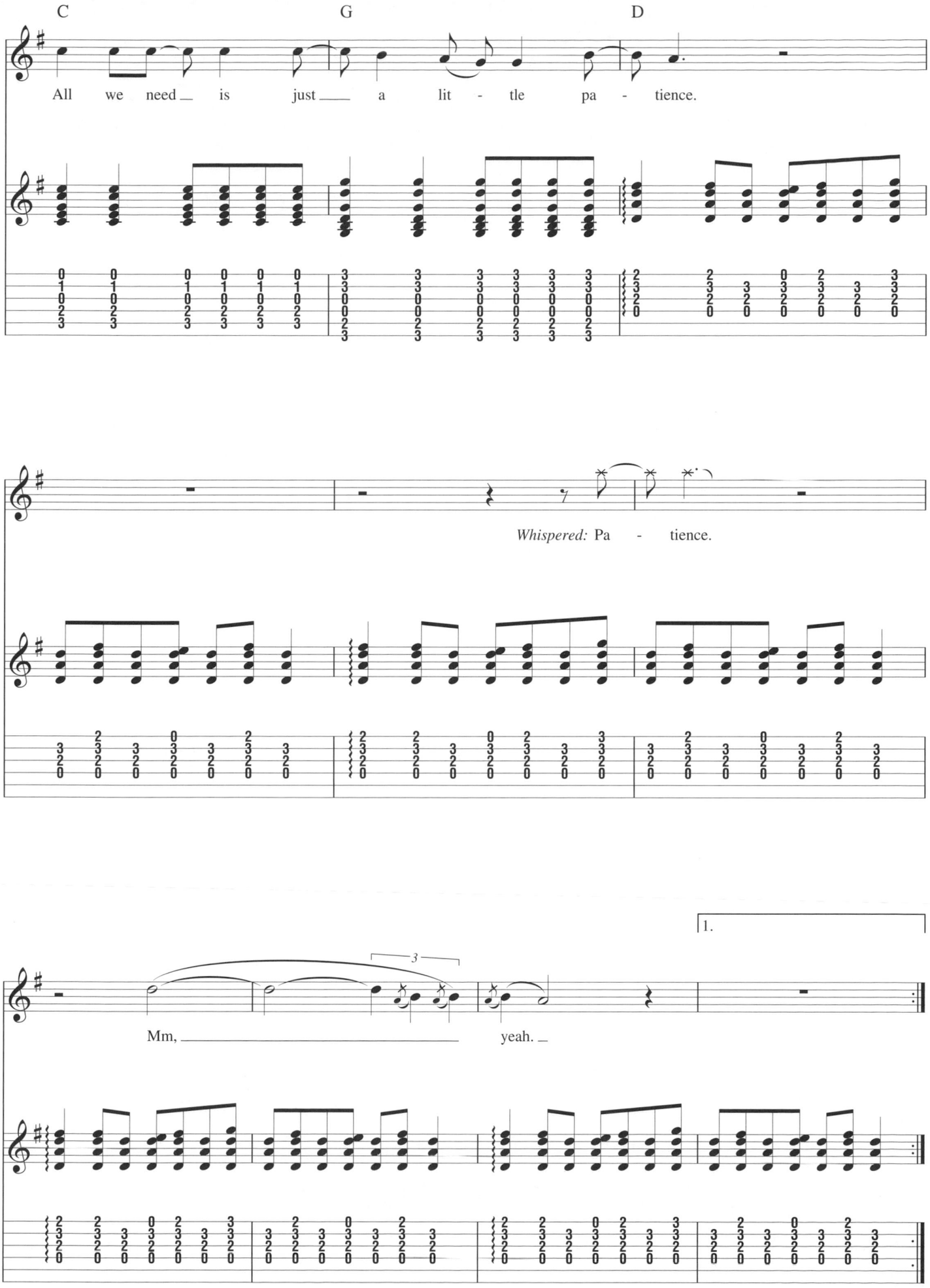
C
G
D
All we need is just a lit - tle pa - tience.
Whispered: Pa - tience.
1.
3
Mm, yeah.

2.
Guitar Solo
C
G
C
Em
C
G
D
D
C
G
C
Em
C
G
D

Outro
Slowly ♩ = 64

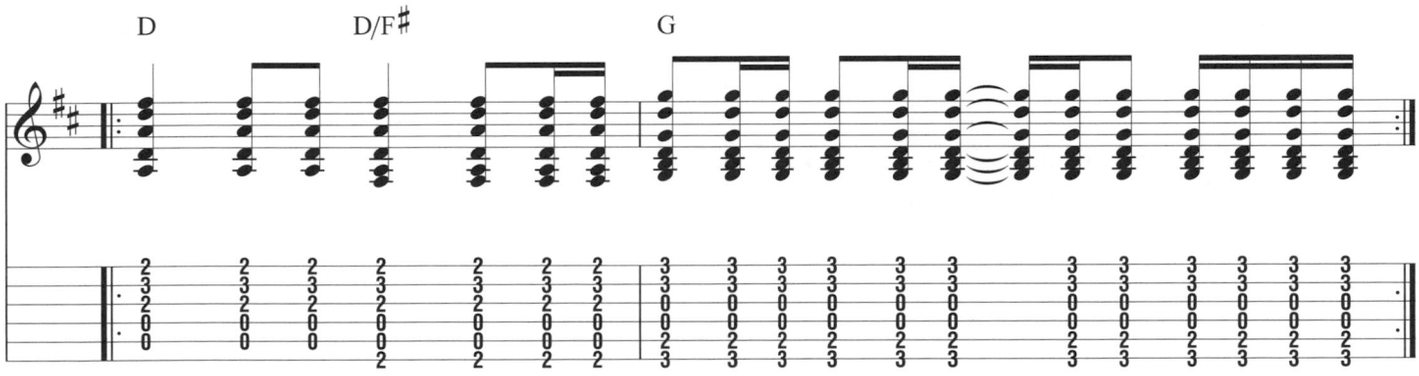

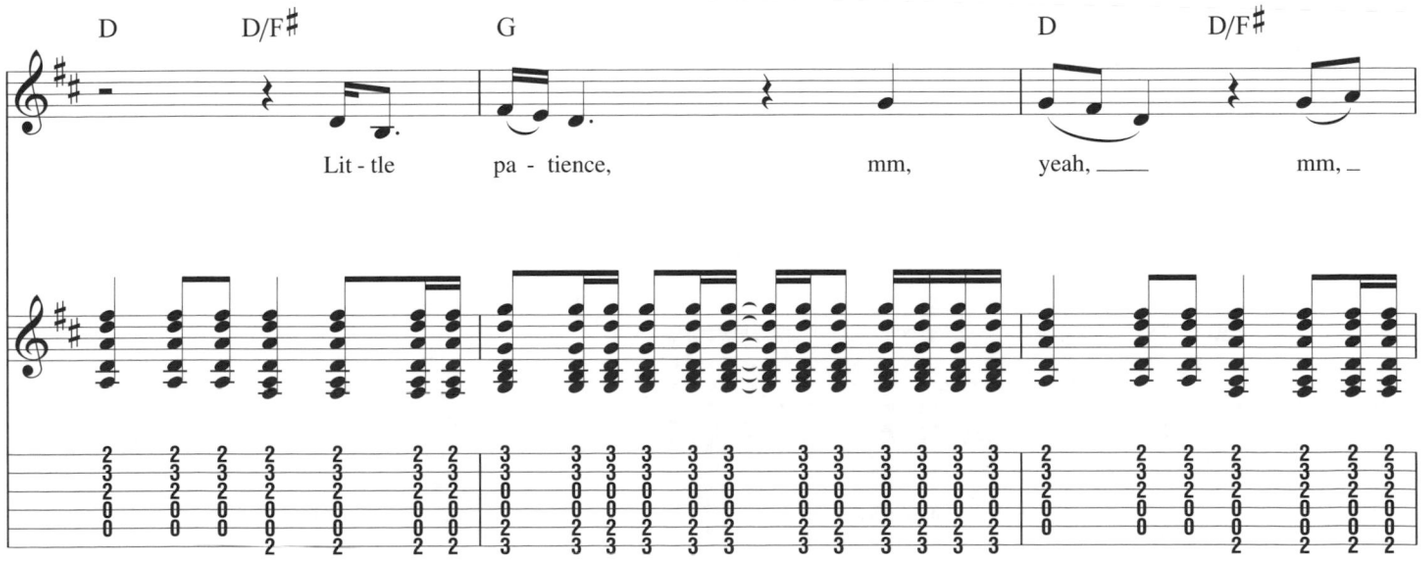

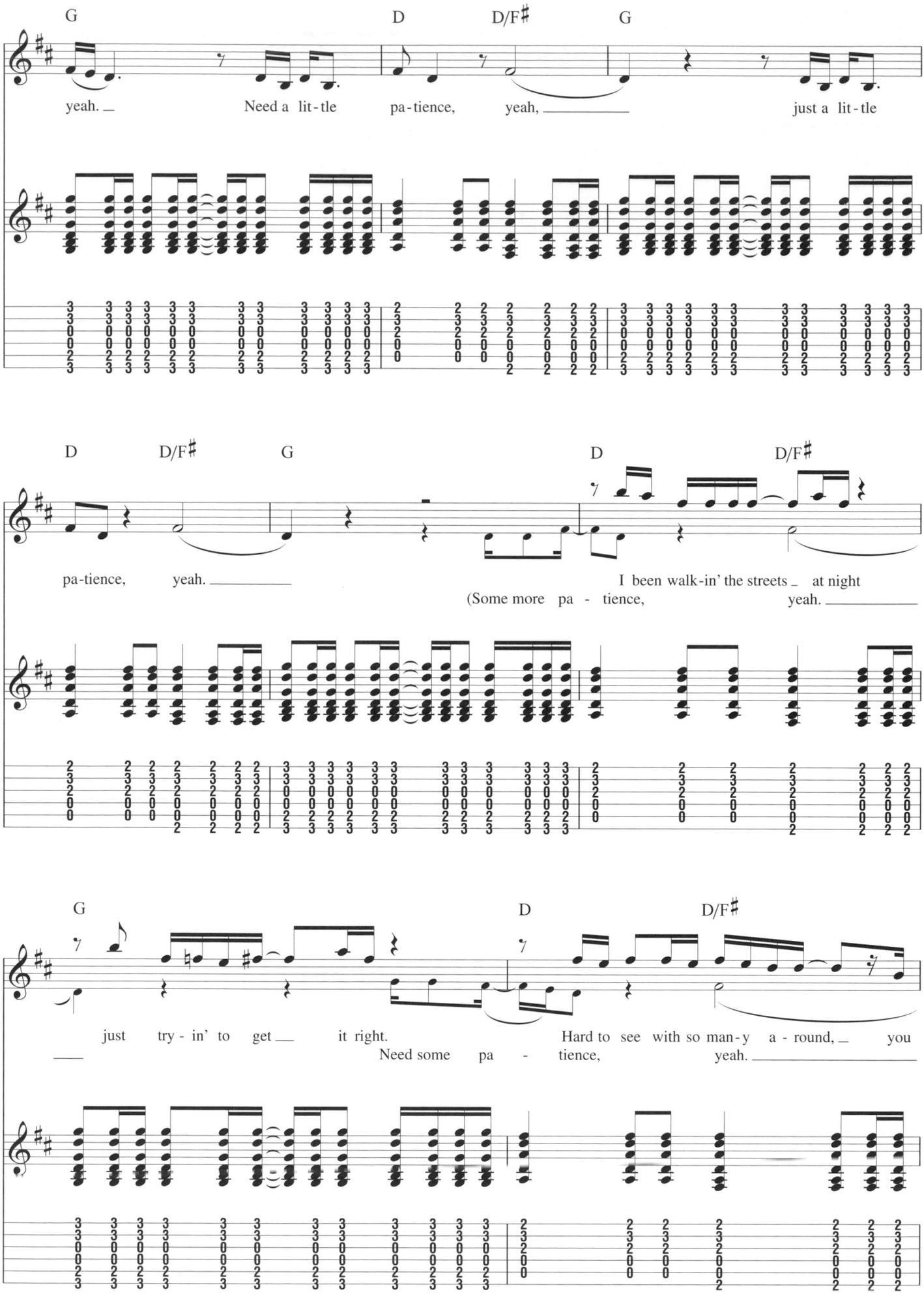
G D D/F♯ G
yeah. Need a lit-tle pa-tience, yeah, just a lit-tle
D D/F♯ G D D/F♯
pa-tience, yeah. I been walk-in' the streets at night
(Some more pa - tience, yeah.
G D D/F♯
just try - in' to get it right. Hard to see with so man-y a - round, you
Need some pa - tience, yeah.

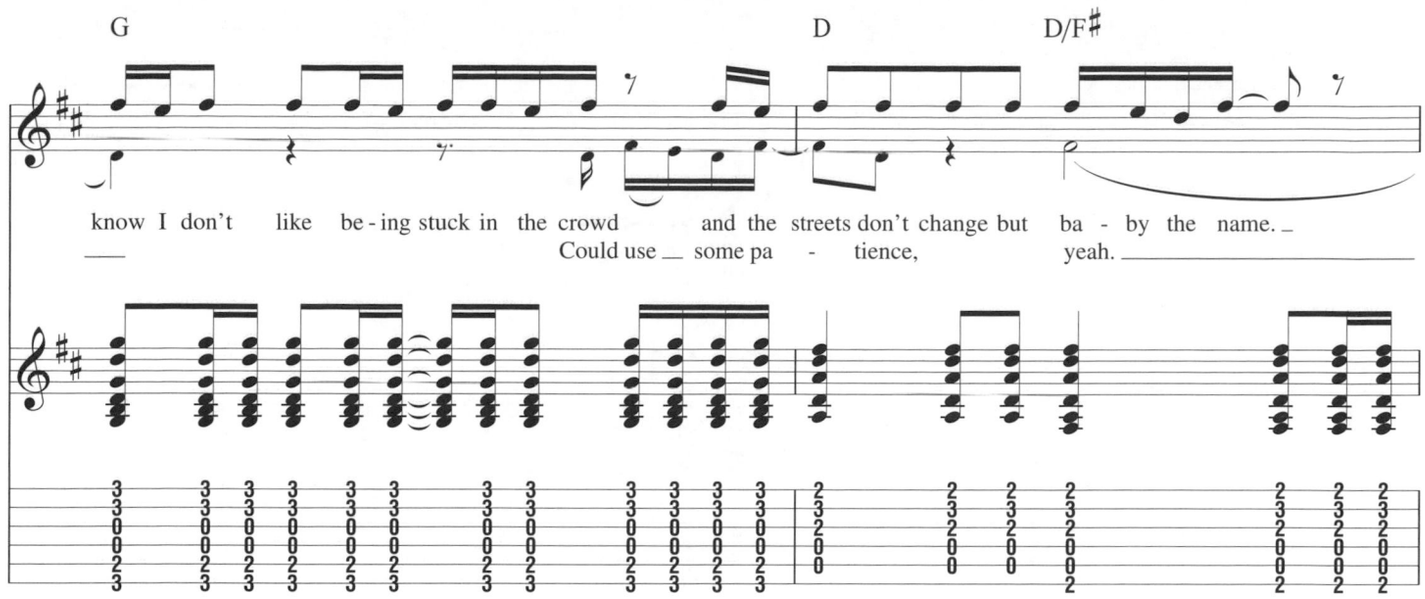
G
D
D/F♯
know I don't like be - ing stuck in the crowd and the streets don't change but ba - by the name.
Could use some pa - tience, yeah.

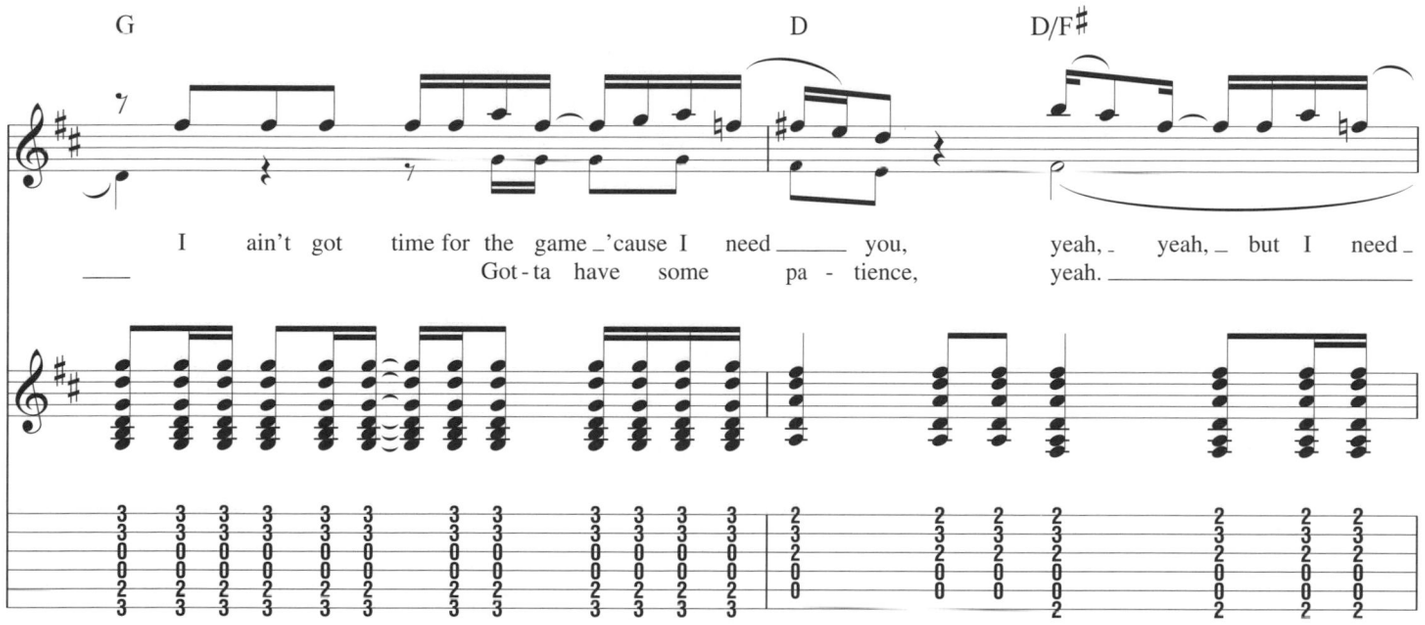
G
D
D/F♯
I ain't got time for the game 'cause I need you, yeah, yeah, but I need
Got - ta have some pa - tience, yeah.

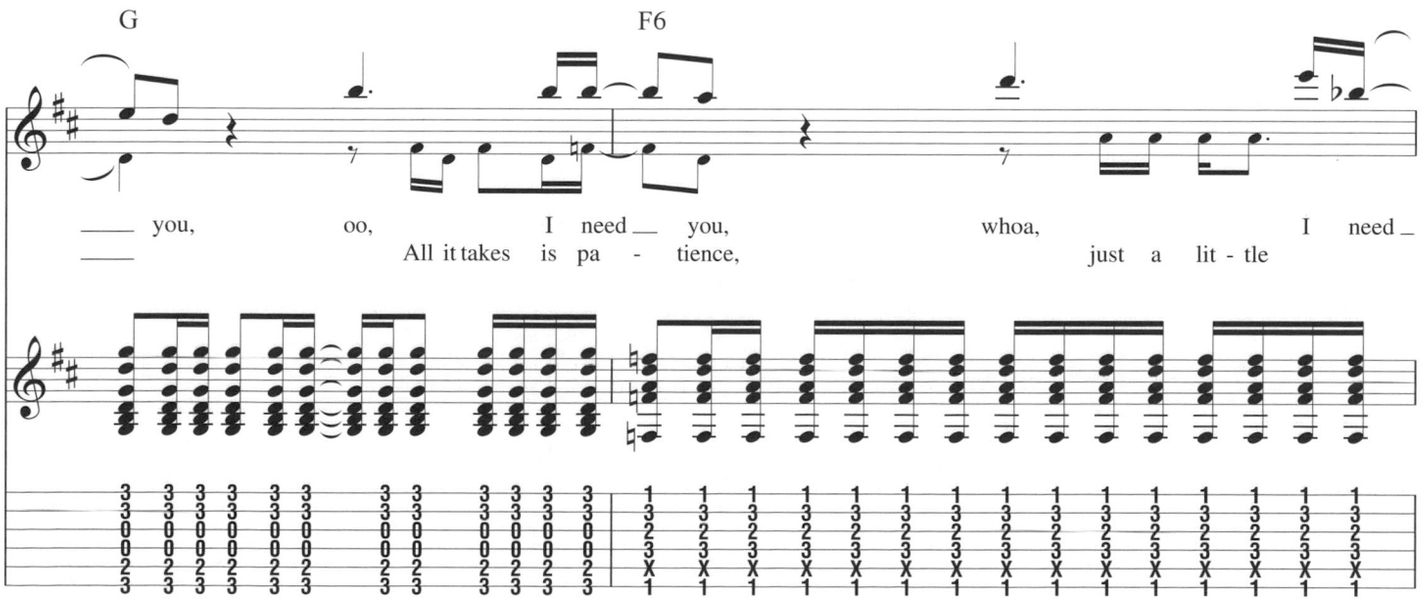
G
F6
you, oo, I need you, whoa, I need
All it takes is pa - tience, just a lit - tle

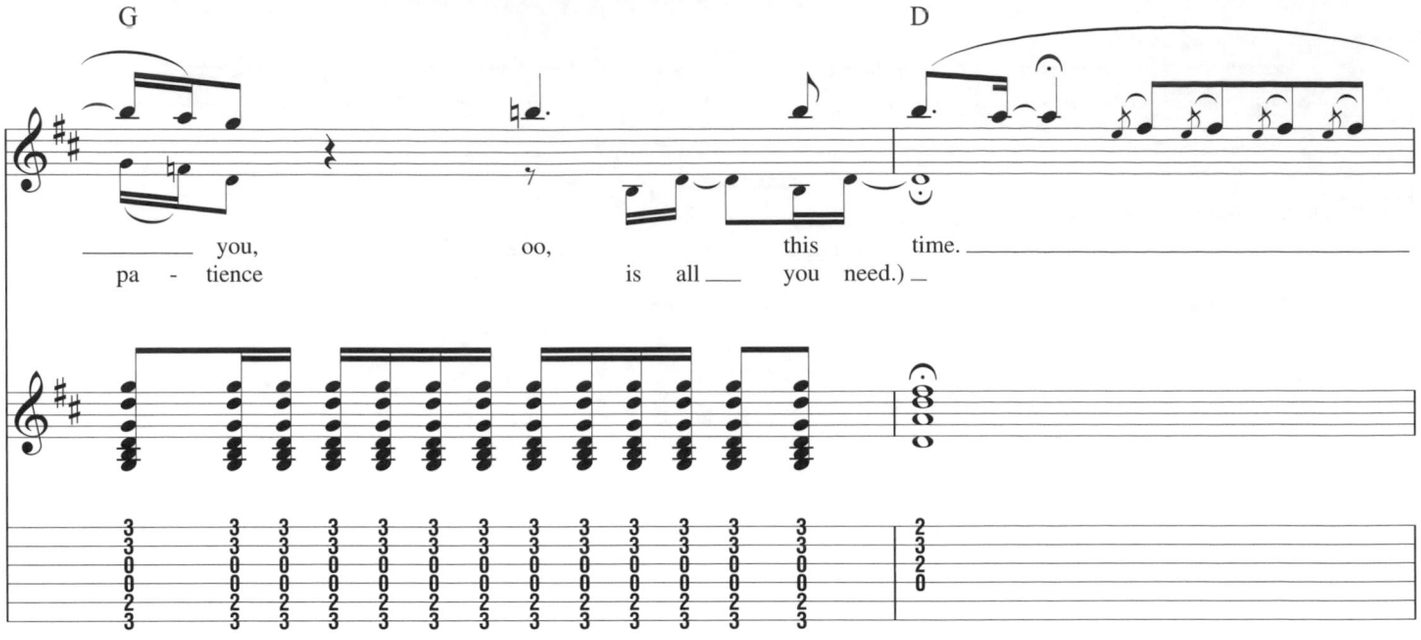

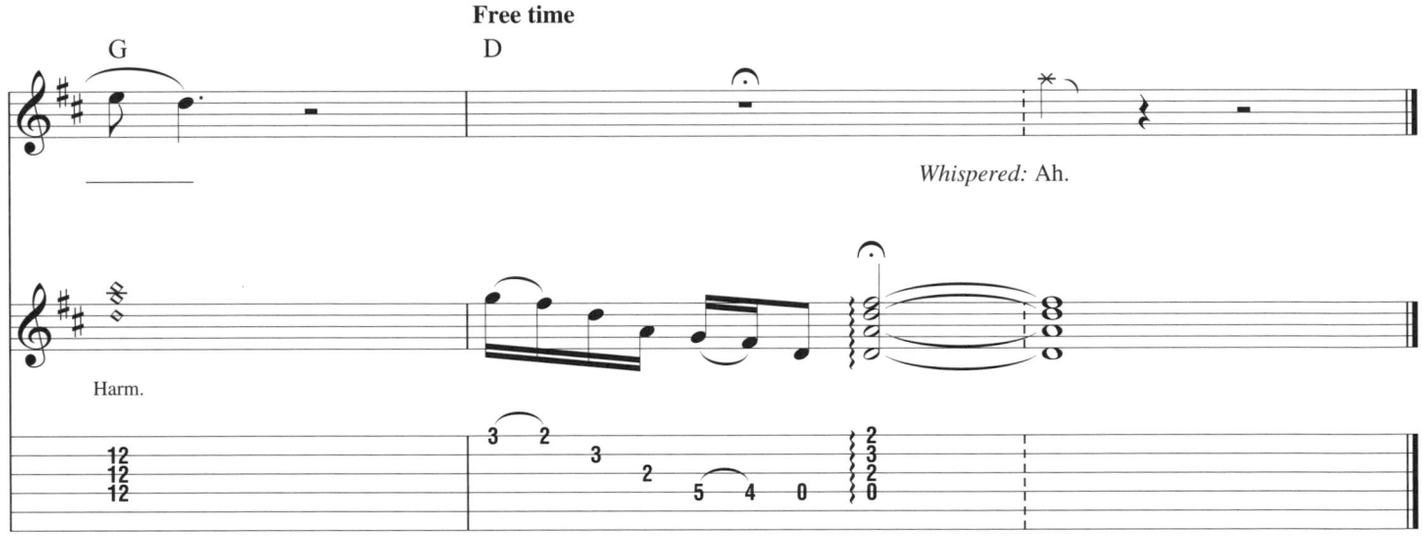

Additional Lyrics

2. I sit here on the stairs 'cause I'd rather be alone.
If I can't have you right now I'll wait, dear.
Sometimes I get so tense but I can't speed up the time.
But you know, love, there's one more thing to consider.

Chorus Said, woman, take it slow and things will be just fine.
You and I'll just use a little patience.
Said, Sugar, take the time 'cause the lights are shining bright.
You and I've got what it takes to make it.
We won't fake it, uh, I'll never break it 'cause I can't take it.

WONDERWALL
Oasis

Video Lesson – 13 minutes, 10 seconds

Standard Tuning: (low to high) E–A–D–G–B–E
Key of A (capo II)

Guitar Tone:

- steel-string acoustic guitar
- capo at 2nd fret

Chords/Arpeggios:

Intro/Verse/Chorus:

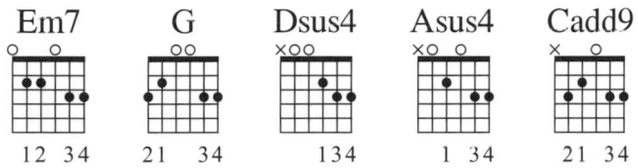

Pre-Chorus:

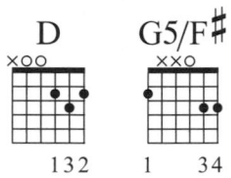

Techniques:

- Strumming: it's not necessary to strum all the notes of each chord every time. Strive for a loose strumming feel, striking only some of the strings within each chord. This will sound more natural and musical. Generally, downstrokes tend to catch the lower three strings and upstrokes catch the higher three strings.
- Common Tones: almost every chord in this song includes the notes D and G on the top two strings. Keep your ring and pinky fingers planted here throughout to make the chord changes nice and smooth while keeping these droning tones constant.
- Arpeggios: in the Pre-Chorus, hold down the full chord shapes for each chord change while you arpeggiate them. Keep your fingers arched so you don't inadvertently mute any strings.

Wonderwall

Words and Music by Noel Gallagher

Capo II

Intro

Moderately slow ♩ = 87

F♯m7 (*Em7) | A (G) | Esus4 (Dsus4) | B7sus4 (A7sus4)

Play 4 times

mf

*Symbols in parentheses represent chord names respective to capoed guitar.
Symbols above reflect actual sounding chords. Capoed fret is "0" in tab.

Verse

F♯m7 (Em7) | A (G) | Esus4 (Dsus4) | B7sus4 (A7sus4)

1. To - day is gon - na be the day that they're gon - na throw it back to you.

F♯m7 (Em7) | A (G) | Esus4 (Dsus4) | B7sus4 (A7sus4)

By now you should have some - how re - al - ized what you got - ta do.

Copyright © 1995 SM Music Publishing UK Limited and Oasis Music
All Rights Administered by Sony/ATV Music Publishing LLC, 424 Church Street, Suite 1200, Nashville, TN 37219
International Copyright Secured All Rights Reserved

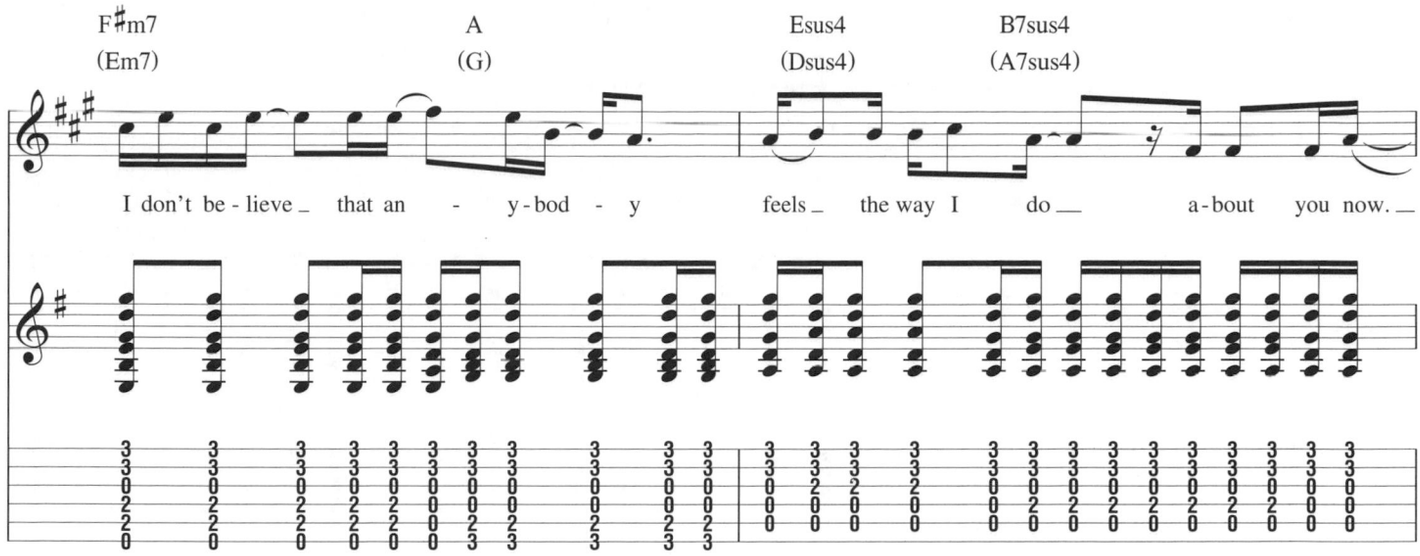
F♯m7
(Em7)
A
(G)
Esus4
(Dsus4)
B7sus4
(A7sus4)
I don't be - lieve _ that an - y - bod - y feels _ the way I do __ a - bout you now. __

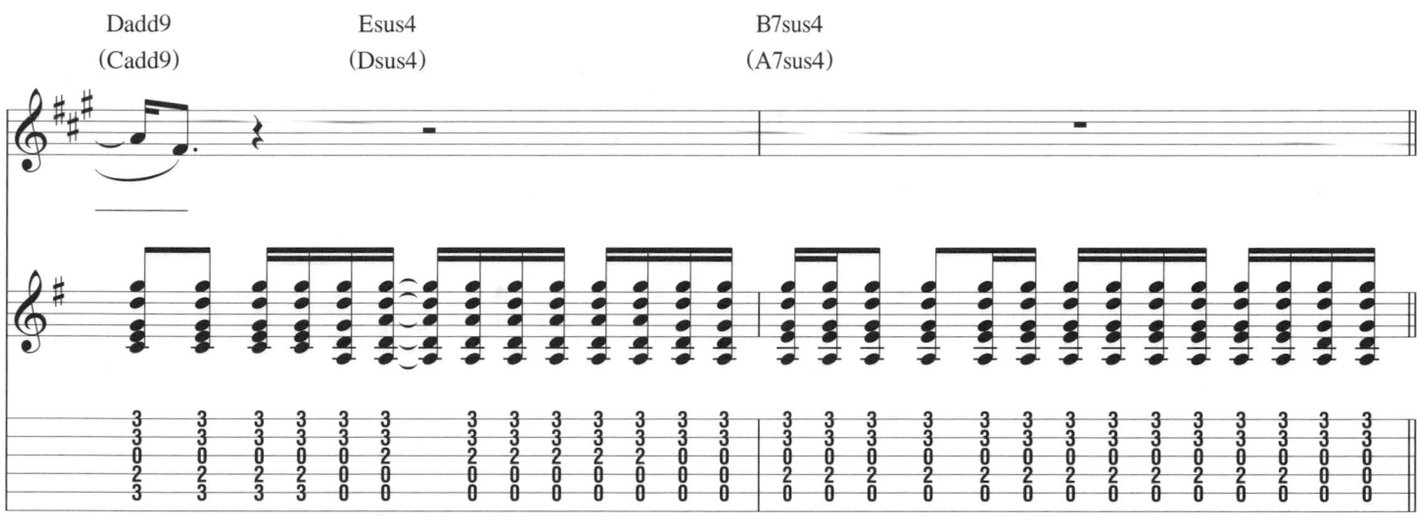
Dadd9
(Cadd9)
Esus4
(Dsus4)
B7sus4
(A7sus4)

Verse

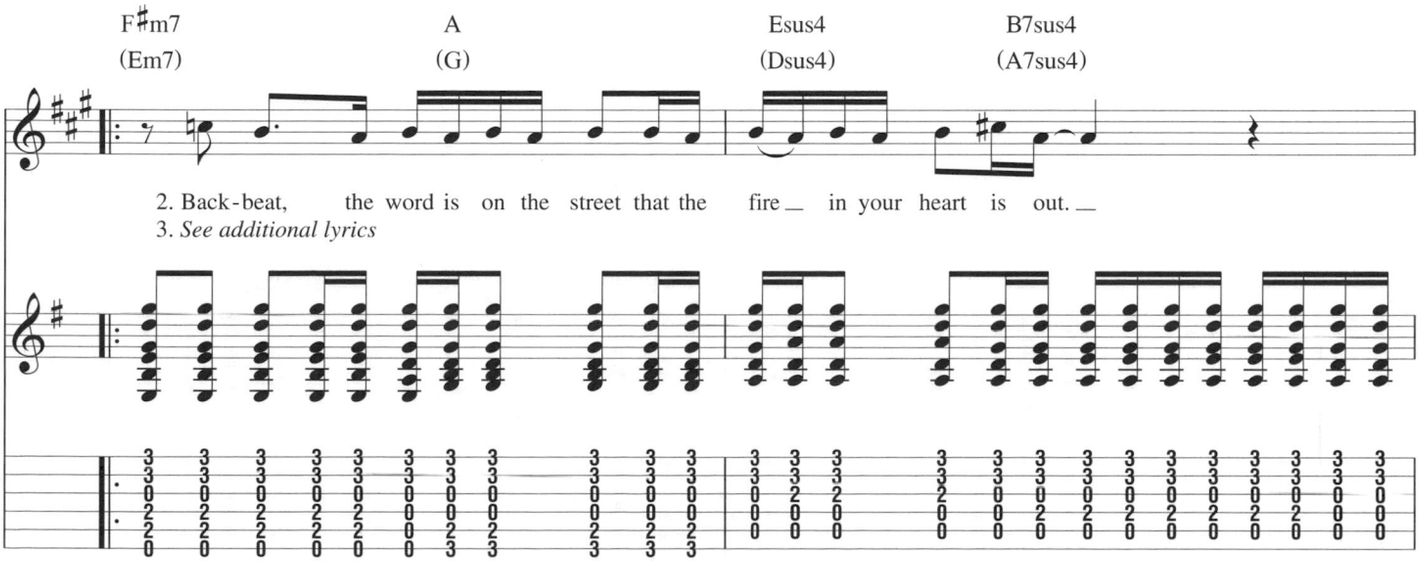
F♯m7
(Em7)
A
(G)
Esus4
(Dsus4)
B7sus4
(A7sus4)
2. Back - beat, the word is on the street that the fire __ in your heart is out. __
3. See additional lyrics

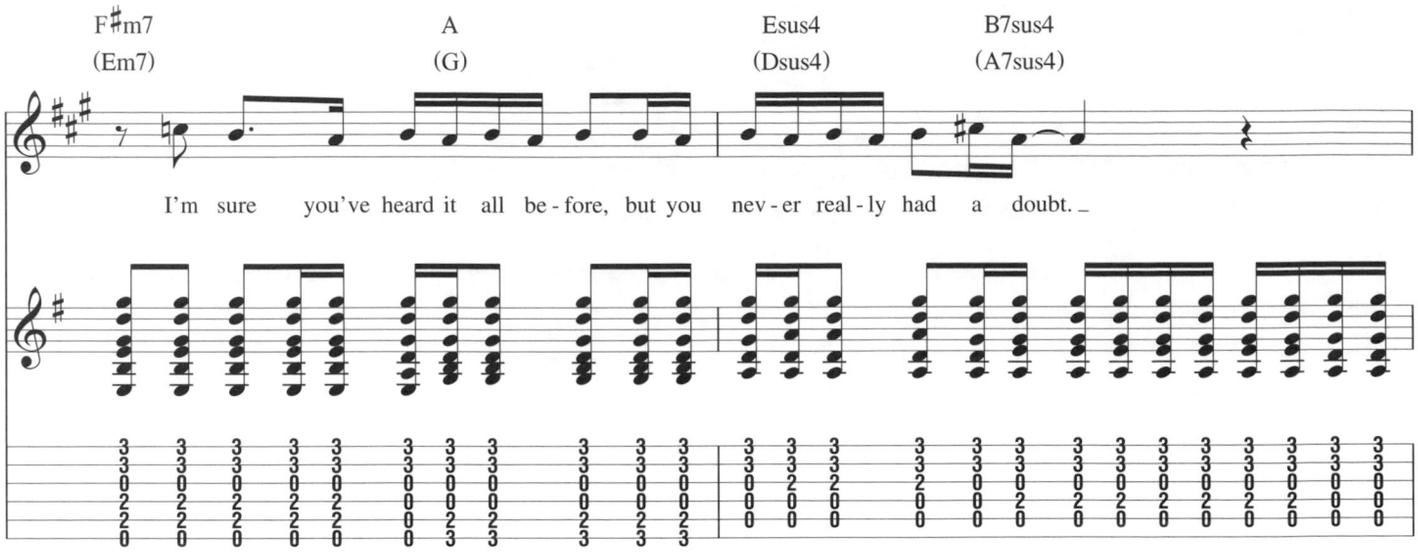
F♯m7
(Em7)
A
(G)
Esus4
(Dsus4)
B7sus4
(A7sus4)
I'm sure you've heard it all be-fore, but you nev-er real-ly had a doubt.

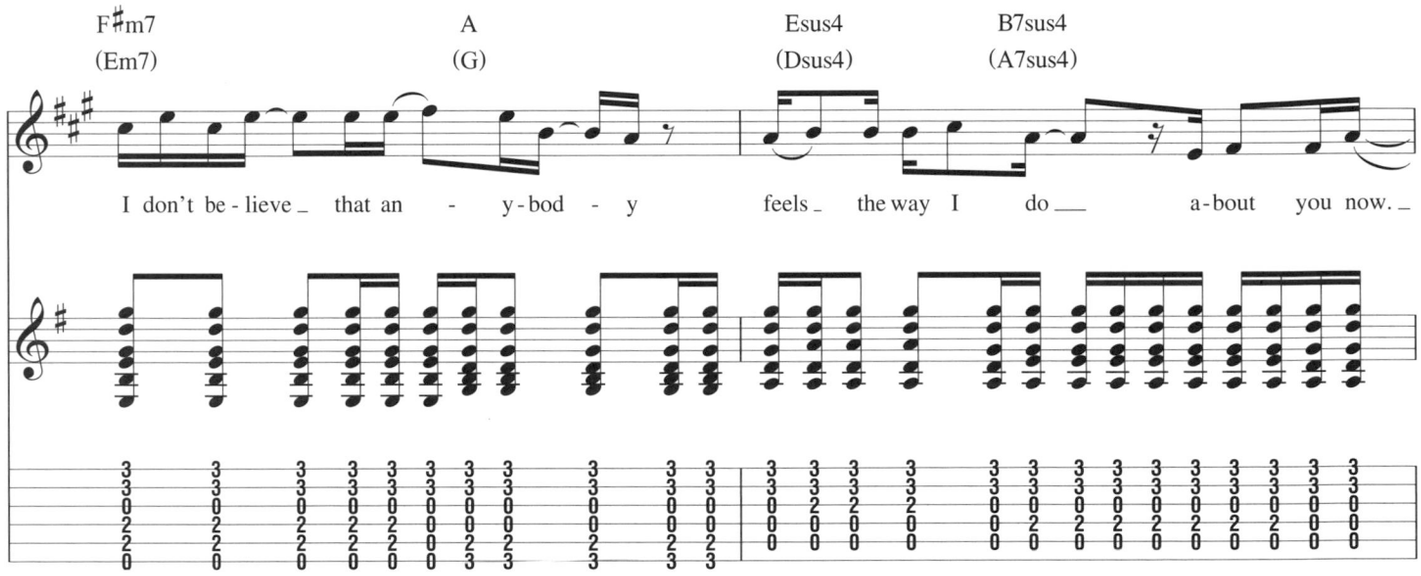
F♯m7
(Em7)
A
(G)
Esus4
(Dsus4)
B7sus4
(A7sus4)
I don't be-lieve that an - y-bod - y feels the way I do a-bout you now.

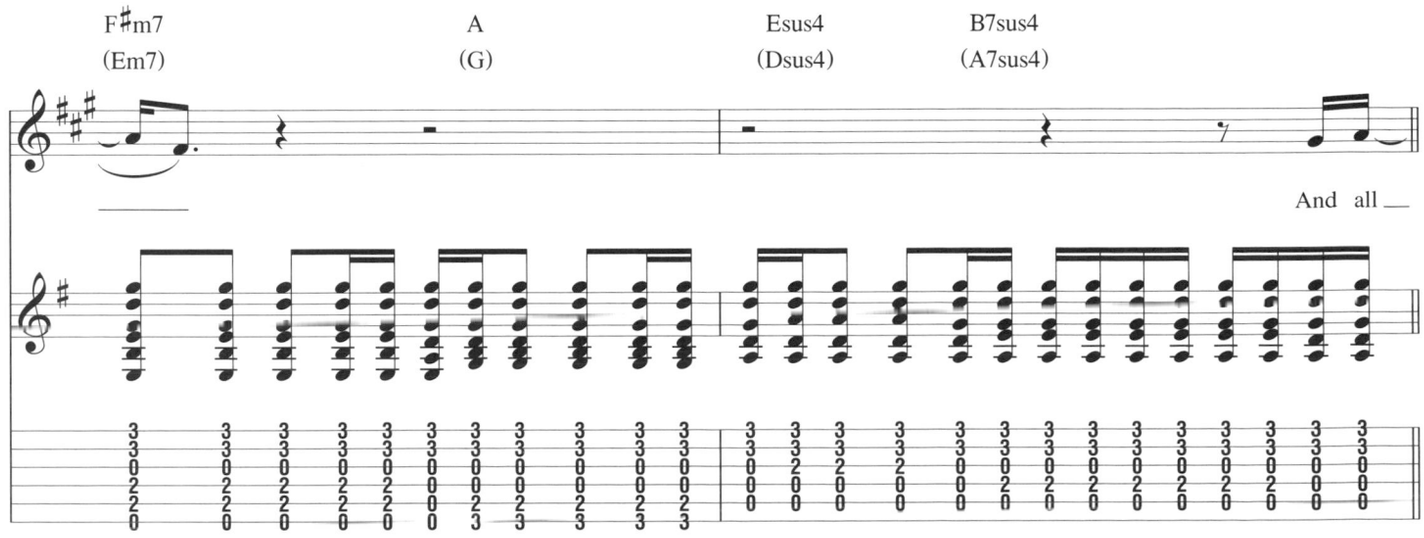
F♯m7
(Em7)
A
(G)
Esus4
(Dsus4)
B7sus4
(A7sus4)
And all

Pre-Chorus
Dadd9 (Cadd9)
E (D)
F♯m7 (Em7)
the roads we have to walk are wind - ing, and all
See additional lyrics
let chords ring throughout
Dadd9 (Cadd9)
E (D)
F♯m7 (Em7)
the lights that lead us there are blind - ing.
Dadd9 (Cadd9)
E (D)
A (G)
A5/G♯ (G5/F♯)
F♯m7 (Em7)
Esus4/A (Dsus4/A)
There are man - y things that I would like to say to you, but I don't know how

B7sus4
(A7sus4)
Be - cause

Chorus

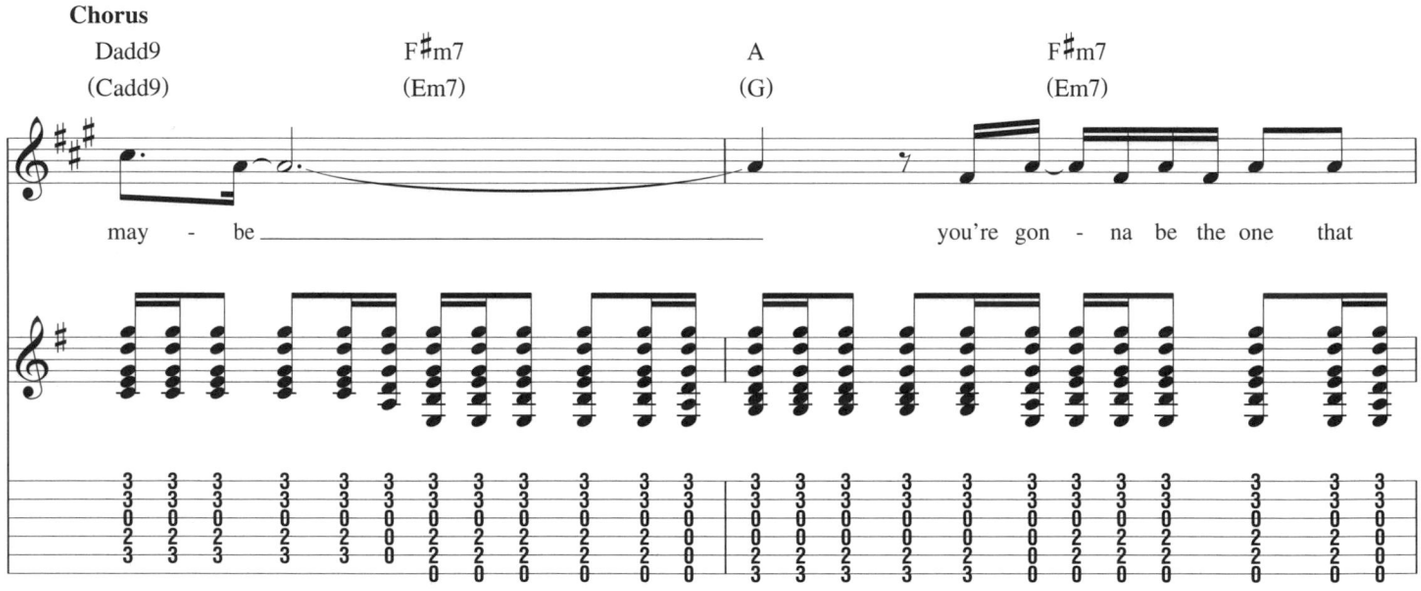
Dadd9
(Cadd9)
F♯m7
(Em7)
A
(G)
F♯m7
(Em7)
may - be
you're gon - na be the one that

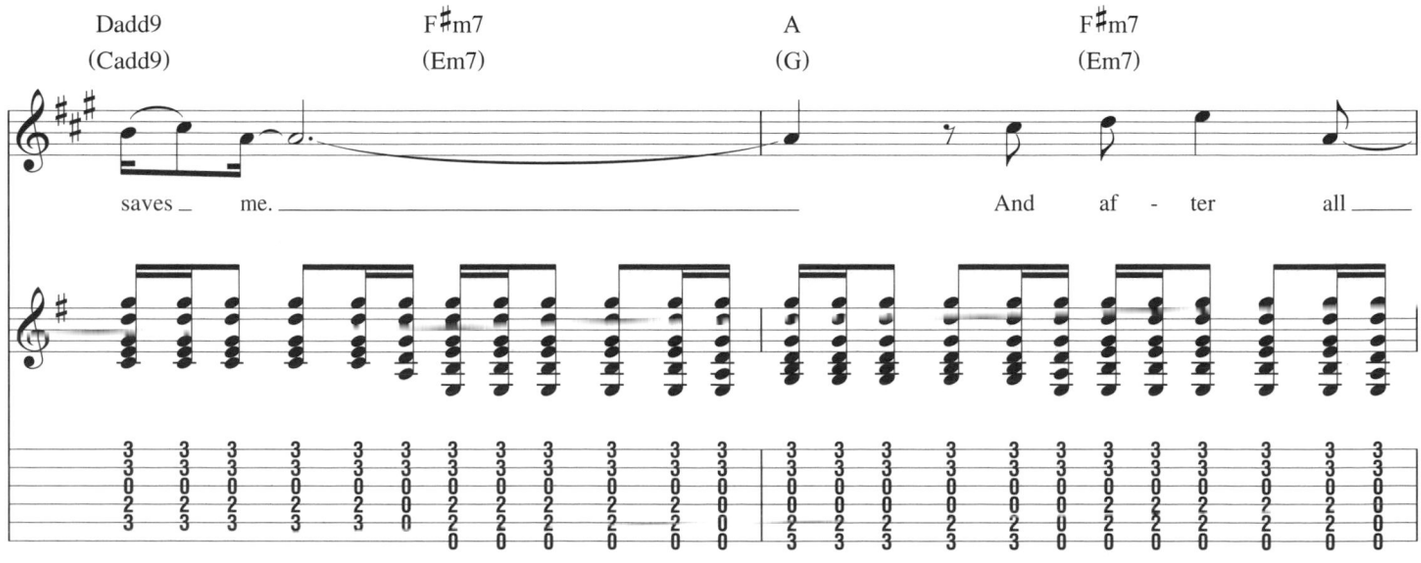
Dadd9
(Cadd9)
F♯m7
(Em7)
A
(G)
F♯m7
(Em7)
saves me.
And af - ter all

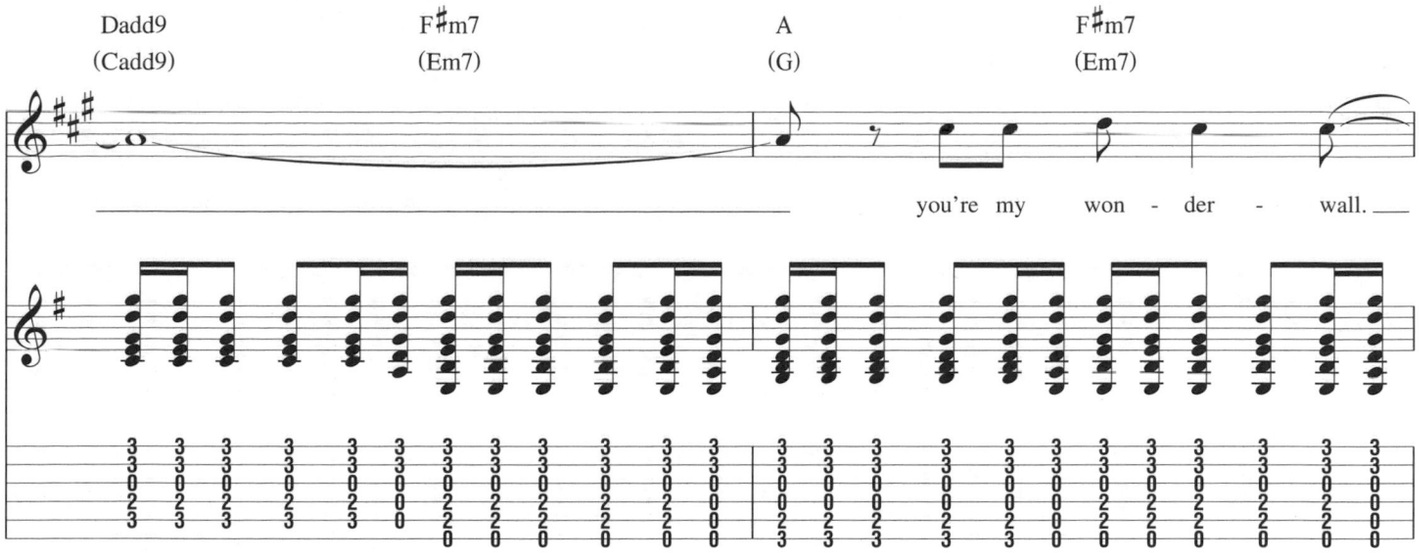
Dadd9
(Cadd9)
F♯m7
(Em7)
A
(G)
F♯m7
(Em7)
you're my won - der - wall.

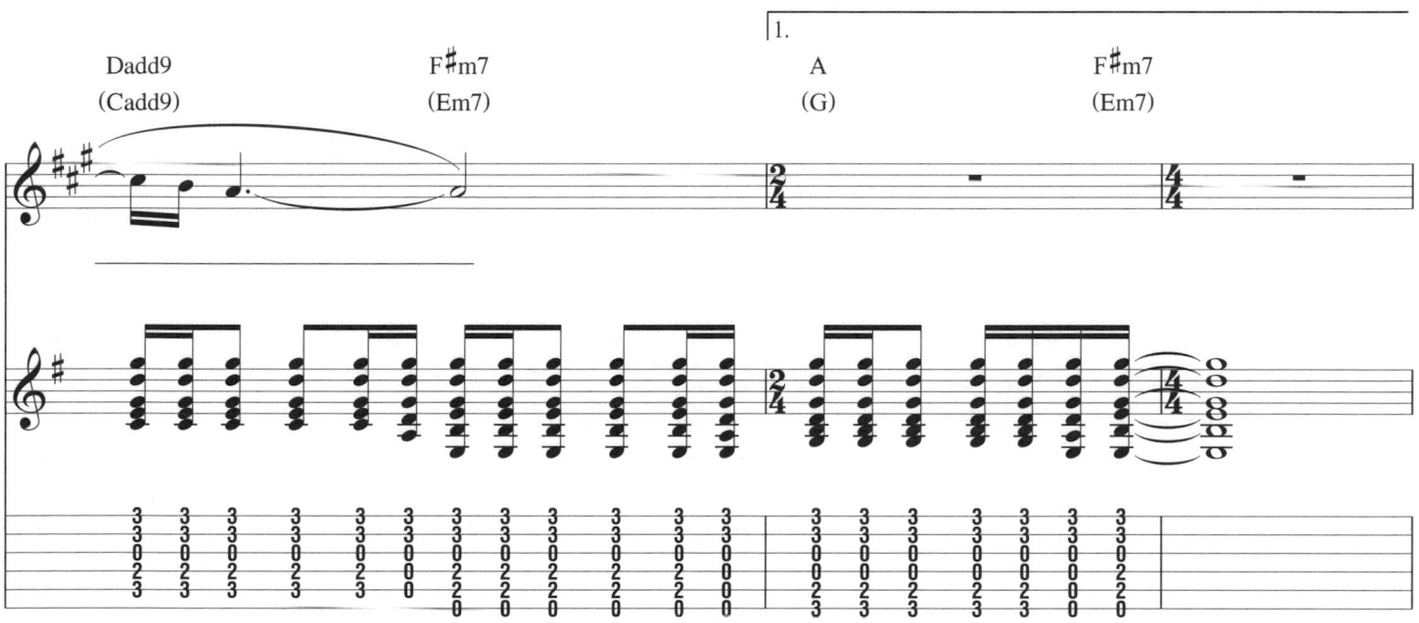
1.
Dadd9
(Cadd9)
F♯m7
(Em7)
A
(G)
F♯m7
(Em7)

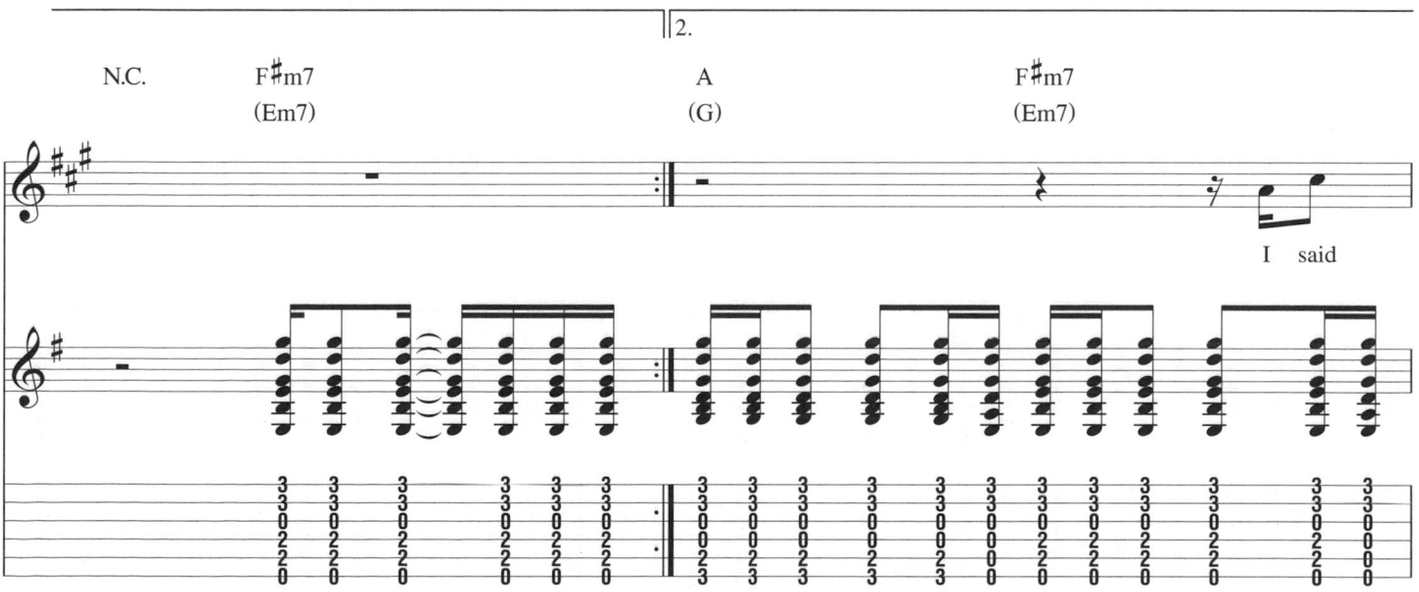
2.
N.C.
F♯m7
(Em7)
A
(G)
F♯m7
(Em7)
I said

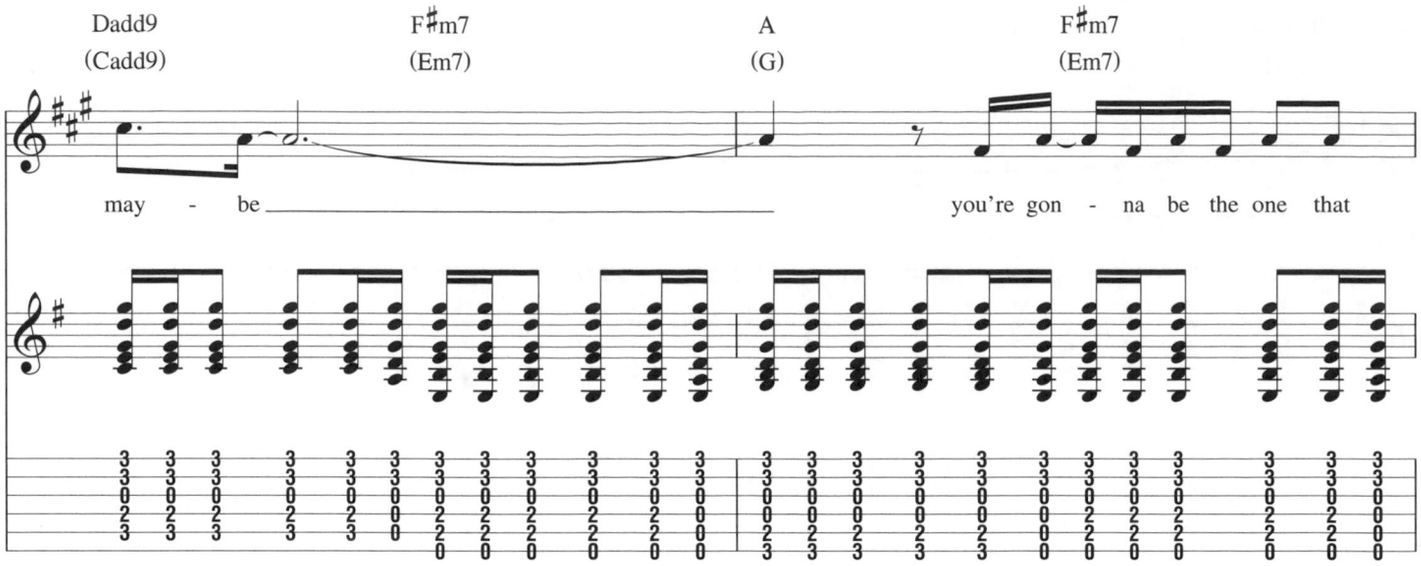
Dadd9
(Cadd9)
F♯m7
(Em7)
A
(G)
F♯m7
(Em7)
may - be
you're gon - na be the one that

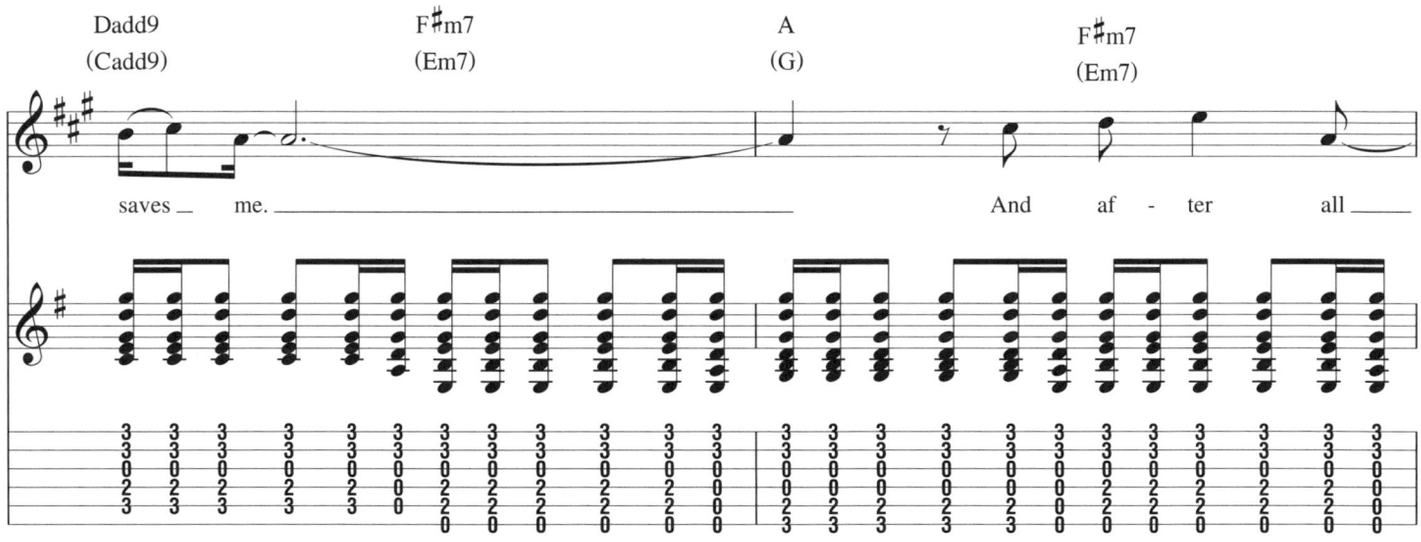
Dadd9
(Cadd9)
F♯m7
(Em7)
A
(G)
F♯m7
(Em7)
saves me.
And af - ter all

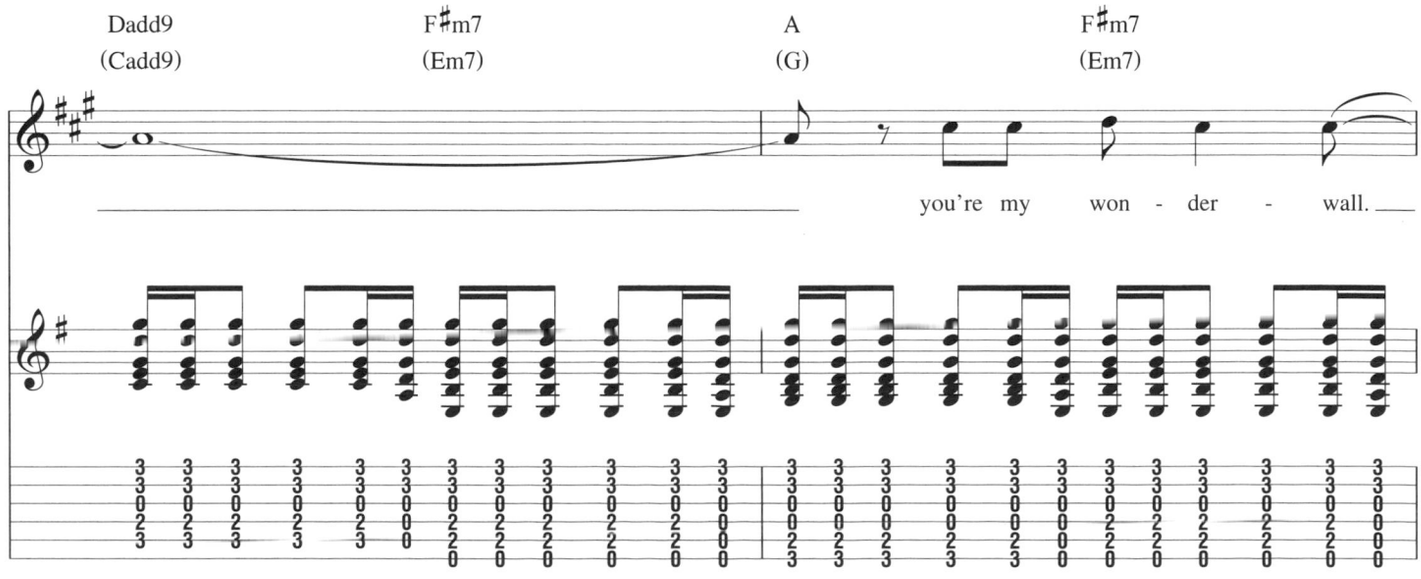
Dadd9
(Cadd9)
F♯m7
(Em7)
A
(G)
F♯m7
(Em7)
you're my won - der - wall.

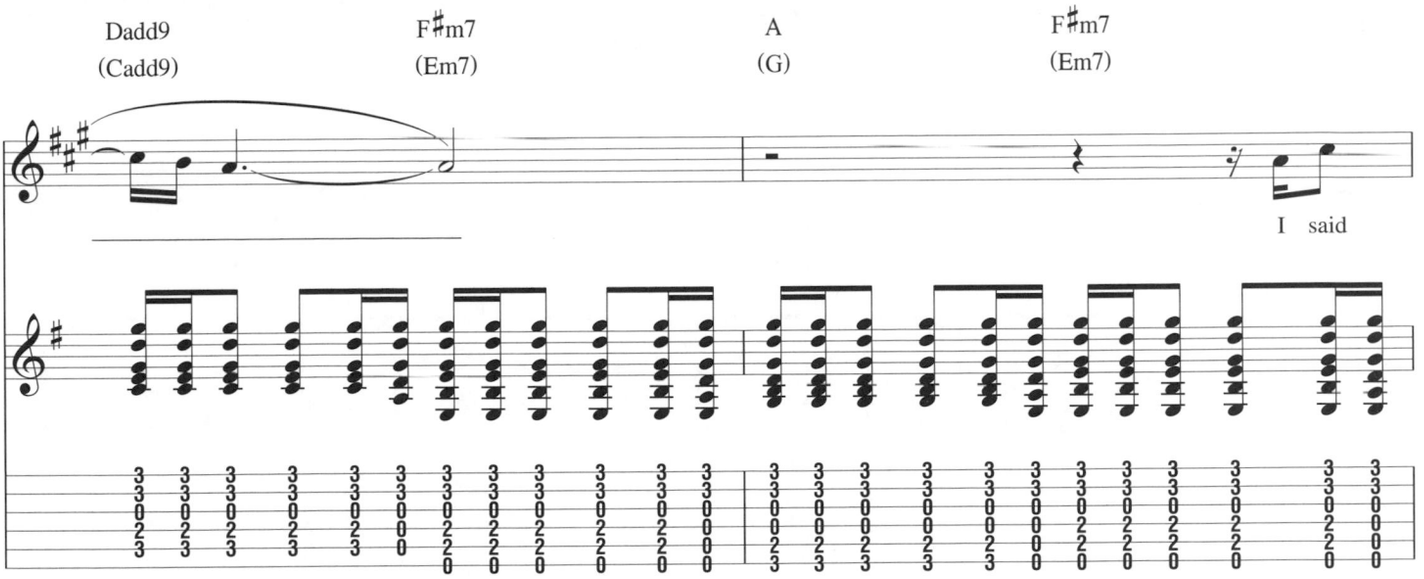
Dadd9
(Cadd9)
F♯m7
(Em7)
A
(G)
F♯m7
(Em7)
I said

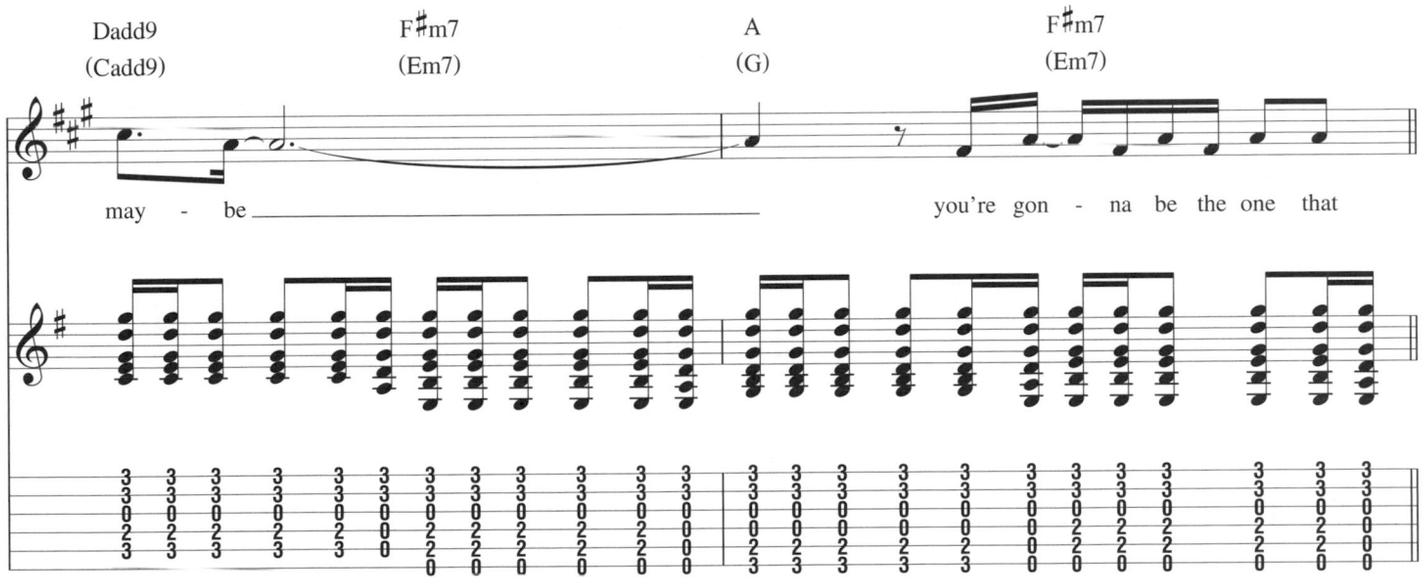
Dadd9
(Cadd9)
F♯m7
(Em7)
A
(G)
F♯m7
(Em7)
may - be
you're gon - na be the one that

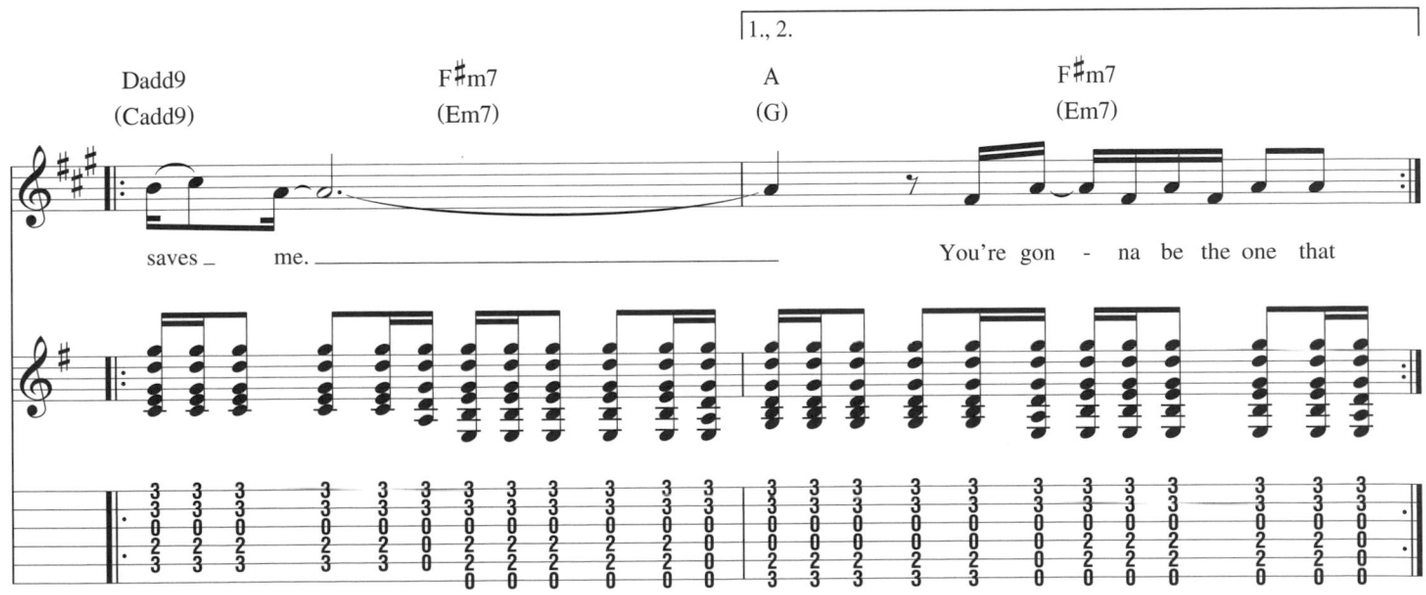
1., 2.
Dadd9
(Cadd9)
F♯m7
(Em7)
A
(G)
F♯m7
(Em7)
saves me.
You're gon - na be the one that

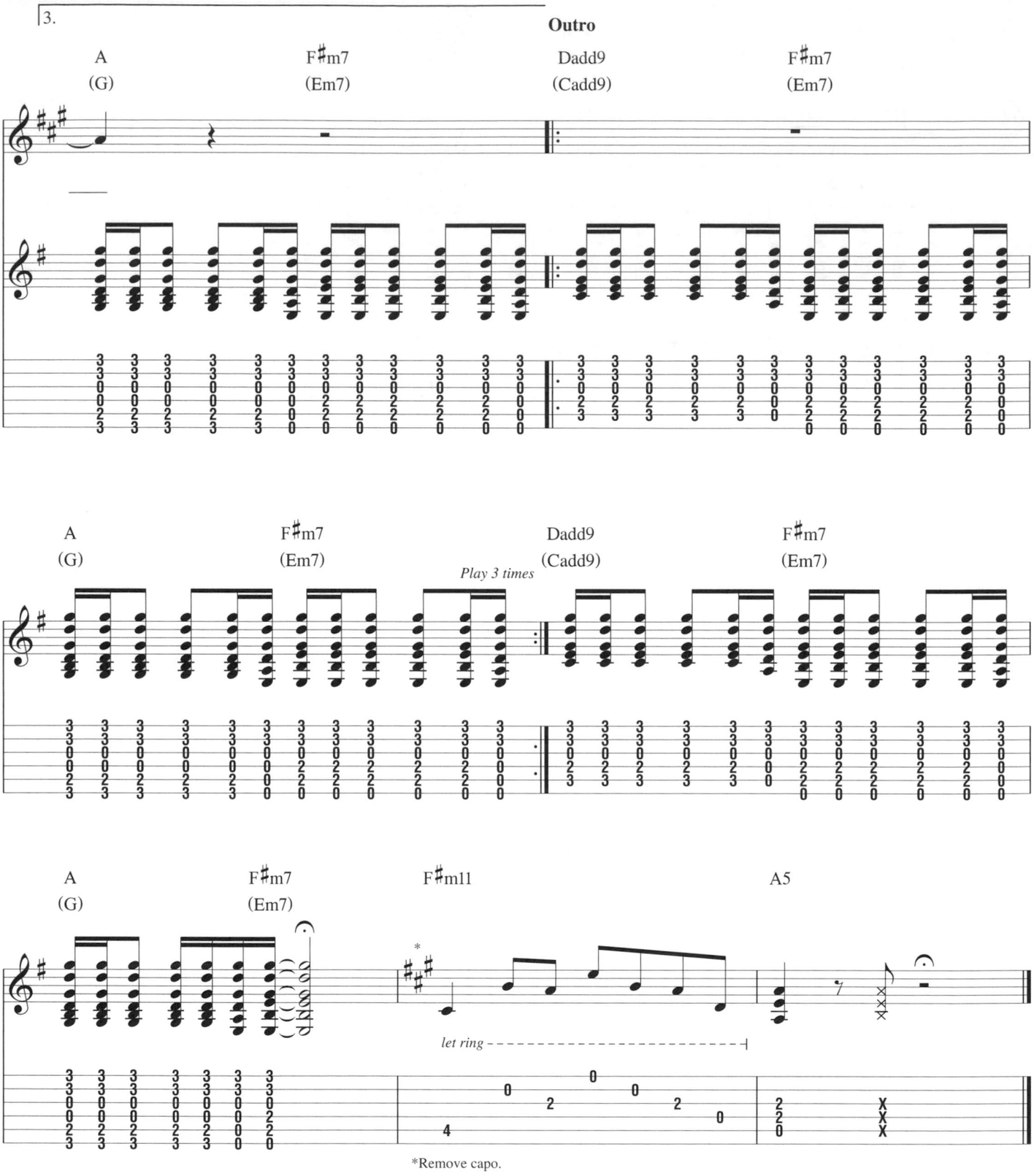

Additional Lyrics

3. Today was gonna be the day, but they'll never throw it back to you.
By now you should have somehow realized what you're not to do.
I don't believe that anybody feels the way I do about you now.

Pre-Chorus And all the roads that lead you there were winding,
And all the lights that light the way are blinding.
There are many things that I would like to say to you,
But I don't know how.
I said...

YOU WERE MEANT FOR ME

Jewel

Video Lesson – 11 minutes, 46 seconds

Tune Down 1/2 Step: (low to high) E♭–A♭–D♭–G♭–B♭–E♭
Key of G

Guitar Tone:

- steel-string acoustic guitar

Chords/Arpeggios:

Intro/Verse:

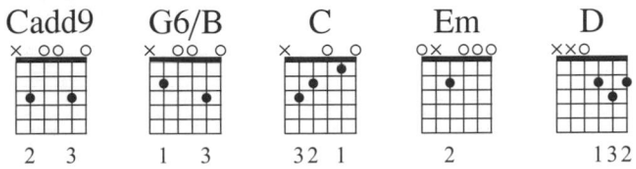

Chorus:

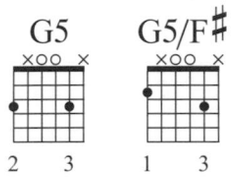

Bridge:

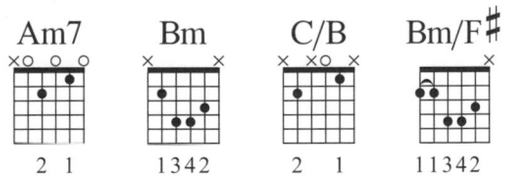

Techniques:

- Fingerpicking: in general, use your thumb to pluck the bass notes on the lower three strings, and your index, middle, and ring fingers to pluck the 3rd, 2nd, and 1st strings, respectively.
- Arpeggios: almost the entire song is arpeggiated, meaning chords are played one note at a time. Keep your fingers arched so you don't inadvertently mute any strings. Strive for a clean, clear attack on each note.
- Shuffle Feel: this song is played with a shuffle feel (or swing feel). This means all 8th notes are played in an uneven, long-short rhythm.
- Fingernails, Flesh, and Fingerpicks: there are several ways you can pluck the strings with your fingers. Fingernails sound great and can provide a consistent, clean attack, but you'll need to keep them well-buffed and filed so they are smooth and curved naturally around the fingertips. Some players will use just the flesh of their fingertips to pluck; this has its advantages as well. The sound is less consistent, but warmer and more organic, plus you don't have the nail maintenance. Another alternative are a thumbpick and fingerpicks, similar to a banjo player. These create a consistent sound and don't require upkeep, but do take some time to get used to.

You Were Meant for Me

Words and Music by Jewel Murray and Steve Poltz

Tune down 1/2 step:
(low to high) E♭-A♭-D♭-G♭-B♭-E♭

Intro
Moderate Folk ♩ = 112 (♫ = ♩ ♪)

Cadd9 G6/B C

mf
w/ fingers
let ring throughout

Em Cadd9 G6/B

C Em

Verse

Cadd9

1. I hear the clock, it's
2., 3. *See additional lyrics*

© 1995, 1996 WIGGLY TOOTH MUSIC and THIRD STORY MUSIC, INC.
All Rights for WIGGLY TOOTH MUSIC Administered by DCTM AVE/DOWNTOWN MUSIC PUBLISHING LLC
Worldwide Rights for THIRD STORY MUSIC, INC. owned by ARC/CONRAD MUSIC LLC
All Rights for ARC/CONRAD MUSIC LLC Administered by BMG RIGHTS MANAGEMENT (US) LLC
All Rights Reserved Used by Permission

G6/B
C
Em
six A. M.
I feel so far from where I've been.
Cadd9
G6/B
C
I got my eggs, I got my pan - cakes too.
I got my ma-ple syr - up, ev-'ry-
D
Cadd9
G6/B
thing but you.
I break the yolks and make a smile - y face.
C
Em
Csus2
I kind - a like it in my brand-new place. Wipe the spots off of the mir'r, don't leave my

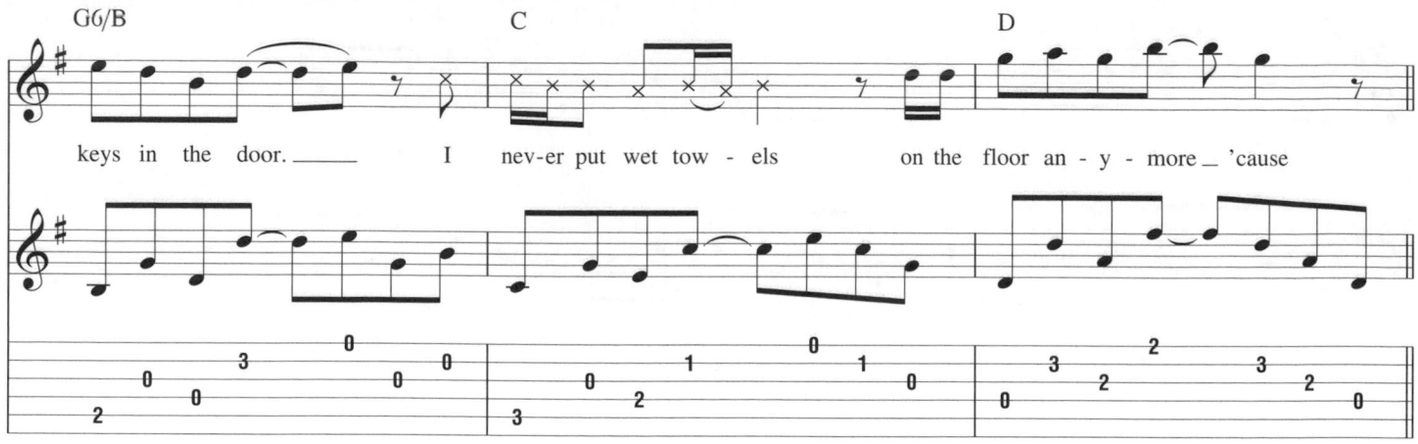
G6/B
C
D
keys in the door. I nev-er put wet tow - els on the floor an - y - more 'cause

Chorus

C
D
G5
G5/F♯
dreams last so long, e - ven af - ter you're gone.

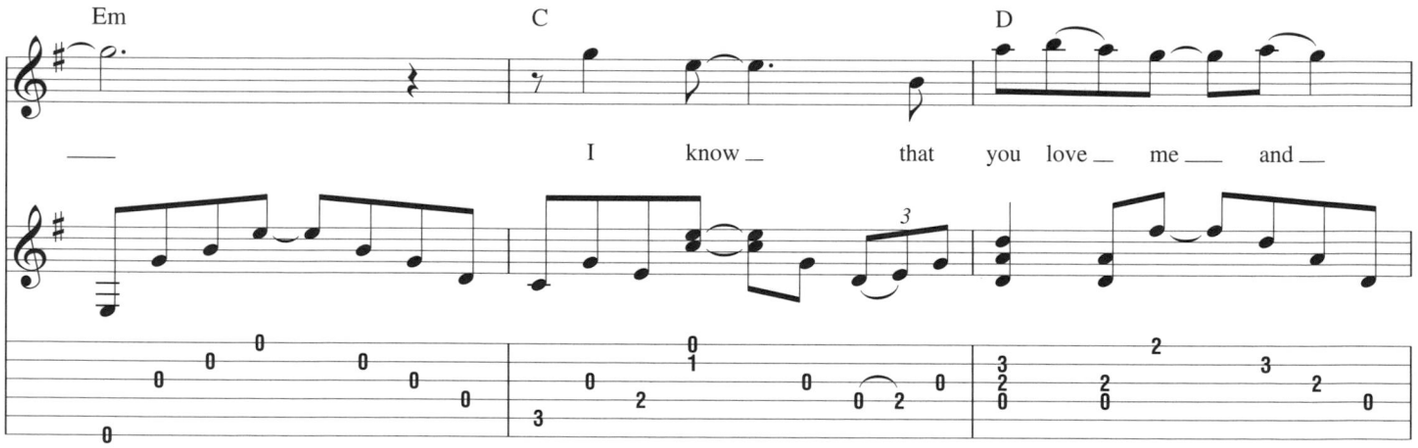
Em
C
D
I know that you love me and

G5
G5/F♯
Em
C
soon you will see you were meant for me and

To Coda
1.
2.
D
Em
Em
I was meant for you.
you.
8va
loco
3
Harm.
Bridge
Am7
D
I go a-bout my bus - 'ness, I'm do - ing fine. Be-sides, a
Bm
D
C
C/B
Am7
what would I say if I had you on the line.
Same old sto - ry, not
D.C. al Coda
D
Bm/F♯
rit.
Em
much to say.
Hearts are bro - ken ev -'ry day.
rit.

Additional Lyrics

2. I called my momma, she was out for a walk.
Consoled a cup of coffee but it didn't wanna talk.
So I picked up the paper, it was more bad news;
More hearts being broken or people being used.
Put on my coat in the pouring rain.
I saw a movie, it just wasn't the same
'Cause it was happy, oh, I was sad
And it made me miss you, oh, so bad 'cause...

3. I brush my teeth, I put the cap back on.
I know you hate it when I leave the light on.
I pick a book up and then I turn the sheets down
And then I take a deep breath and a good look around.
Put on my PJs and hop into bed.
I'm half alive but I feel mostly dead.
I try and tell myself it'll all be alright.
I just shouldn't think anymore tonight 'cause...

GUITAR NOTATION LEGEND

THE MUSICAL STAFF shows pitches and rhythms and is divided by bar lines into measures. Pitches are named after the first seven letters of the alphabet.

TABLATURE graphically represents the guitar fingerboard. Each horizontal line represents a string, and each number represents a fret.

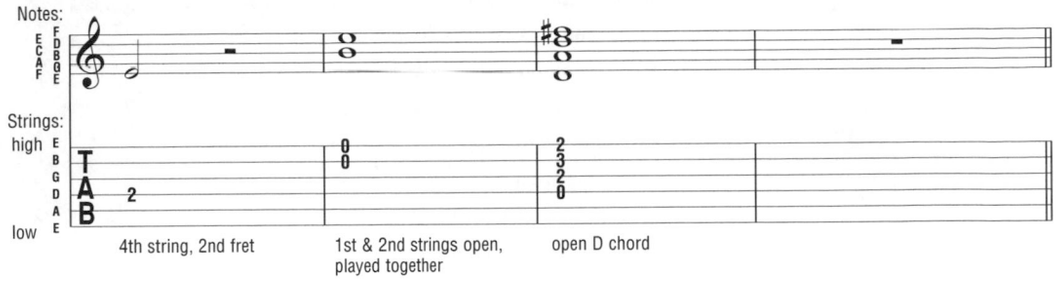

HALF-STEP BEND: Strike the note and bend up 1/2 step.

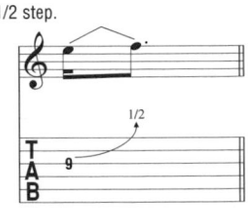

WHOLE-STEP BEND: Strike the note and bend up one step.

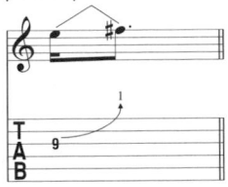

GRACE NOTE BEND: Strike the note and immediately bend up as indicated.

SLIGHT (MICROTONE) BEND: Strike the note and bend up 1/4 step.

BEND AND RELEASE: Strike the note and bend up as indicated, then release back to the original note. Only the first note is struck.

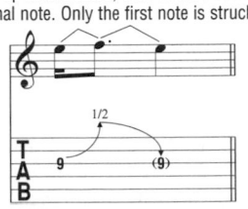

PRE-BEND: Bend the note as indicated, then strike it.

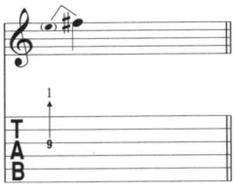

VIBRATO: The string is vibrated by rapidly bending and releasing the note with the fretting hand.

PALM MUTING: The note is partially muted by the pick hand lightly touching the string(s) just before the bridge.

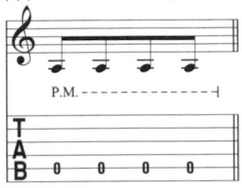

HAMMER-ON: Strike the first (lower) note with one finger, then sound the higher note (on the same string) with another finger by fretting it without picking.

PULL-OFF: Place both fingers on the notes to be sounded. Strike the first note and without picking, pull the finger off to sound the second (lower) note.

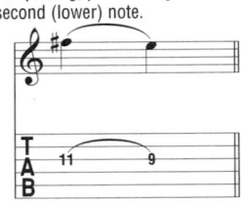

LEGATO SLIDE: Strike the first note and then slide the same fret-hand finger up or down to the second note. The second note is not struck.

SHIFT SLIDE: Same as legato slide, except the second note is struck.

TRILL: Very rapidly alternate between the notes indicated by continuously hammering on and pulling off.

TAPPING: Hammer ("tap") the fret indicated with the pick-hand index or middle finger and pull off to the note fretted by the fret hand.

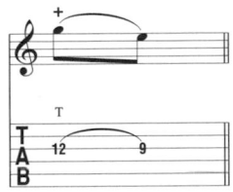

NATURAL HARMONIC: Strike the note while the fret-hand lightly touches the string directly over the fret indicated.

PINCH HARMONIC: The note is fretted normally and a harmonic is produced by adding the edge of the thumb or the tip of the index finger of the pick hand to the normal pick attack.

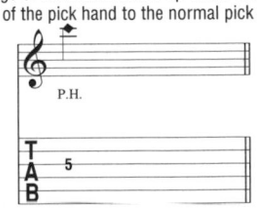

TREMOLO PICKING: The note is picked as rapidly and continuously as possible.

VIBRATO BAR DIVE AND RETURN: The pitch of the note or chord is dropped a specified number of steps (in rhythm), then returned to the original pitch.

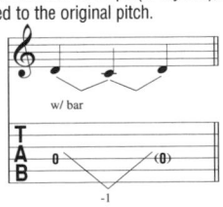

VIBRATO BAR SCOOP: Depress the bar just before striking the note, then quickly release the bar.

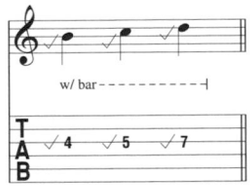

VIBRATO BAR DIP: Strike the note and then immediately drop a specified number of steps, then release back to the original pitch.

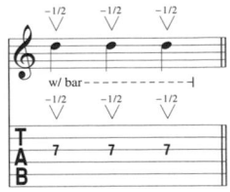

Additional Musical Definitions

(accent) • Accentuate note (play it louder).

(staccato) • Play the note short.

D.S. al Coda • Go back to the sign (𝄋), then play until the measure marked "***To Coda***," then skip to the section labelled "**Coda**."

D.C. al Fine • Go back to the beginning of the song and play until the measure marked "***Fine***" (end).

Fill • Label used to identify a brief melodic figure which is to be inserted into the arrangement.

N.C. • Harmony is implied.

• Repeat measures between signs.

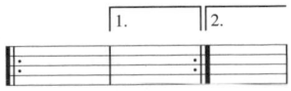

• When a repeated section has different endings, play the first ending only the first time and the second ending only the second time.

HAL•LEONARD GUITAR PLAY-ALONG®

This series will help you play your favorite songs quickly and easily. Just follow the tab and listen to the audio to the hear how the guitar should sound, and then play along using the separate backing tracks. Mac or PC users can also slow down the tempo without changing pitch by using the CD in their computer. The melody and lyrics are included in the book so that you can sing or simply follow along.

INCLUDES TAB

VOL. 1 – ROCK	00699570 / $16.99
VOL. 2 – ACOUSTIC	00699569 / $16.95
VOL. 3 – HARD ROCK	00699573 / $16.95
VOL. 4 – POP/ROCK	00699571 / $16.99
VOL. 5 – MODERN ROCK	00699574 / $16.99
VOL. 6 – '90S ROCK	00699572 / $16.99
VOL. 7 – BLUES	00699575 / $16.95
VOL. 8 – ROCK	00699585 / $14.99
VOL. 10 – ACOUSTIC	00699586 / $16.95
VOL. 11 – EARLY ROCK	00699579 / $14.95
VOL. 12 – POP/ROCK	00699587 / $14.95
VOL. 13 – FOLK ROCK	00699581 / $15.99
VOL. 14 – BLUES ROCK	00699582 / $16.95
VOL. 15 – R&B	00699583 / $14.95
VOL. 16 – JAZZ	00699584 / $15.95
VOL. 17 – COUNTRY	00699588 / $15.95
VOL. 18 – ACOUSTIC ROCK	00699577 / $15.95
VOL. 19 – SOUL	00699578 / $14.99
VOL. 20 – ROCKABILLY	00699580 / $14.95
VOL. 21 – YULETIDE	00699602 / $14.95
VOL. 22 – CHRISTMAS	00699600 / $15.95
VOL. 23 – SURF	00699635 / $14.95
VOL. 24 – ERIC CLAPTON	00699649 / $17.99
VOL. 25 – LENNON & MCCARTNEY	00699642 / $16.99
VOL. 26 – ELVIS PRESLEY	00699643 / $14.95
VOL. 27 – DAVID LEE ROTH	00699645 / $16.95
VOL. 28 – GREG KOCH	00699646 / $14.95
VOL. 29 – BOB SEGER	00699647 / $15.99
VOL. 30 – KISS	00699644 / $16.99
VOL. 31 – CHRISTMAS HITS	00699652 / $14.95
VOL. 32 – THE OFFSPRING	00699653 / $14.95
VOL. 33 – ACOUSTIC CLASSICS	00699656 / $16.95
VOL. 34 – CLASSIC ROCK	00699658 / $16.95
VOL. 35 – HAIR METAL	00699660 / $16.95
VOL. 36 – SOUTHERN ROCK	00699661 / $16.95
VOL. 37 – ACOUSTIC UNPLUGGED	00699662 / $22.99
VOL. 38 – BLUES	00699663 / $16.95
VOL. 39 – '80S METAL	00699664 / $16.99
VOL. 40 – INCUBUS	00699668 / $17.95
VOL. 41 – ERIC CLAPTON	00699669 / $16.95
VOL. 42 – 2000S ROCK	00699670 / $16.99
VOL. 43 – LYNYRD SKYNYRD	00699681 / $17.95
VOL. 44 – JAZZ	00699689 / $14.99
VOL. 45 – TV THEMES	00699718 / $14.95
VOL. 46 – MAINSTREAM ROCK	00699722 / $16.95
VOL. 47 – HENDRIX SMASH HITS	00699723 / $19.95
VOL. 48 – AEROSMITH CLASSICS	00699724 / $17.99
VOL. 49 – STEVIE RAY VAUGHAN	00699725 / $17.99
VOL. 50 – VAN HALEN 1978-1984	00110269 / $17.99
VOL. 51 – ALTERNATIVE '90S	00699727 / $14.99
VOL. 52 – FUNK	00699728 / $14.95
VOL. 53 – DISCO	00699729 / $14.99
VOL. 54 – HEAVY METAL	00699730 / $14.95
VOL. 55 – POP METAL	00699731 / $14.95
VOL. 56 – FOO FIGHTERS	00699749 / $15.99
VOL. 57 – SYSTEM OF A DOWN	00699751 / $14.95
VOL. 58 – BLINK-182	00699772 / $14.95
VOL. 59 – CHET ATKINS	00702347 / $16.99
VOL. 60 – 3 DOORS DOWN	00699774 / $14.95
VOL. 61 – SLIPKNOT	00699775 / $16.99
VOL. 62 – CHRISTMAS CAROLS	00699798 / $12.95
VOL. 63 – CREEDENCE CLEARWATER REVIVAL	00699802 / $16.99
VOL. 64 – THE ULTIMATE OZZY OSBOURNE	00699803 / $16.99
VOL. 66 – THE ROLLING STONES	00699807 / $16.95
VOL. 67 – BLACK SABBATH	00699808 / $16.99
VOL. 68 – PINK FLOYD – DARK SIDE OF THE MOON	00699809 / $16.99
VOL. 69 – ACOUSTIC FAVORITES	00699810 / $14.95
VOL. 70 – OZZY OSBOURNE	00699805 / $16.99
VOL. 71 – CHRISTIAN ROCK	00699824 / $14.95
VOL. 73 – BLUESY ROCK	00699829 / $16.99
VOL. 75 – TOM PETTY	00699882 / $16.99
VOL. 76 – COUNTRY HITS	00699884 / $14.95
VOL. 77 – BLUEGRASS	00699910 / $14.99
VOL. 78 – NIRVANA	00700132 / $16.99
VOL. 79 – NEIL YOUNG	00700133 / $24.99
VOL. 80 – ACOUSTIC ANTHOLOGY	00700175 / $19.95
VOL. 81 – ROCK ANTHOLOGY	00700176 / $22.99
VOL. 82 – EASY SONGS	00700177 / $12.99
VOL. 83 – THREE CHORD SONGS	00700178 / $16.99
VOL. 84 – STEELY DAN	00700200 / $16.99
VOL. 85 – THE POLICE	00700269 / $16.99
VOL. 86 – BOSTON	00700465 / $16.99
VOL. 87 – ACOUSTIC WOMEN	00700763 / $14.99
VOL. 88 – GRUNGE	00700467 / $16.99
VOL. 89 – REGGAE	00700468 / $15.99
VOL. 90 – CLASSICAL POP	00700469 / $14.99
VOL. 91 – BLUES INSTRUMENTALS	00700505 / $14.99
VOL. 92 – EARLY ROCK INSTRUMENTALS	00700506 / $14.99
VOL. 93 – ROCK INSTRUMENTALS	00700507 / $16.99
VOL. 94 – SLOW BLUES	00700508 / $16.99
VOL. 95 – BLUES CLASSICS	00700509 / $14.99
VOL. 96 – THIRD DAY	00700560 / $14.95
VOL. 97 – ROCK BAND	00700703 / $14.99
VOL. 99 – ZZ TOP	00700762 / $16.99
VOL. 100 – B.B. KING	00700466 / $16.99
VOL. 101 – SONGS FOR BEGINNERS	00701917 / $14.99
VOL. 102 – CLASSIC PUNK	00700769 / $14.99
VOL. 103 – SWITCHFOOT	00700773 / $16.99
VOL. 104 – DUANE ALLMAN	00700846 / $16.99
VOL. 105 – LATIN	00700939 / $16.99
VOL. 106 – WEEZER	00700958 / $14.99
VOL. 107 – CREAM	00701069 / $16.99
VOL. 108 – THE WHO	00701053 / $16.99
VOL. 109 – STEVE MILLER	00701054 / $14.99
VOL. 110 – SLIDE GUITAR HITS	00701055 / $16.99
VOL. 111 – JOHN MELLENCAMP	00701056 / $14.99
VOL. 112 – QUEEN	00701052 / $16.99
VOL. 113 – JIM CROCE	00701058 / $15.99
VOL. 114 – BON JOVI	00701060 / $14.99
VOL. 115 – JOHNNY CASH	00701070 / $16.99
VOL. 116 – THE VENTURES	00701124 / $14.99
VOL. 117 – BRAD PAISLEY	00701224 / $16.99
VOL. 118 – ERIC JOHNSON	00701353 / $16.99
VOL. 119 – AC/DC CLASSICS	00701356 / $17.99
VOL. 120 – PROGRESSIVE ROCK	00701457 / $14.99
VOL. 121 – U2	00701508 / $16.99
VOL. 122 – CROSBY, STILLS & NASH	00701610 / $16.99
VOL. 123 – LENNON & MCCARTNEY ACOUSTIC	00701614 / $16.99
VOL. 125 – JEFF BECK	00701687 / $16.99
VOL. 126 – BOB MARLEY	00701701 / $16.99
VOL. 127 – 1970S ROCK	00701739 / $14.99
VOL. 128 – 1960S ROCK	00701740 / $14.99
VOL. 129 – MEGADETH	00701741 / $16.99
VOL. 131 – 1990S ROCK	00701743 / $14.99
VOL. 132 – COUNTRY ROCK	00701757 / $15.99
VOL. 133 – TAYLOR SWIFT	00701894 / $16.99
VOL. 134 – AVENGED SEVENFOLD	00701906 / $16.99
VOL. 136 – GUITAR THEMES	00701922 / $14.99
VOL. 137 – IRISH TUNES	00701966 / $15.99
VOL. 138 – BLUEGRASS CLASSICS	00701967 / $14.99
VOL. 139 – GARY MOORE	00702370 / $16.99
VOL. 140 – MORE STEVIE RAY VAUGHAN	00702396 / $17.99
VOL. 141 – ACOUSTIC HITS	00702401 / $16.99
VOL. 143 – SLASH	00702425 / $19.99
VOL. 144 – DJANGO REINHARDT	00702531 / $16.99
VOL. 145 – DEF LEPPARD	00702532 / $16.99
VOL. 146 – ROBERT JOHNSON	00702533 / $16.99
VOL. 147 – SIMON & GARFUNKEL	14041591 / $16.99
VOL. 148 – BOB DYLAN	14041592 / $16.99
VOL. 149 – AC/DC HITS	14041593 / $17.99
VOL. 150 – ZAKK WYLDE	02501717 / $16.99
VOL. 152 – JOE BONAMASSA	02501751 / $19.99
VOL. 153 – RED HOT CHILI PEPPERS	00702990 / $19.99
VOL. 155 – ERIC CLAPTON – FROM THE ALBUM UNPLUGGED	00703085 / $16.99
VOL. 156 – SLAYER	00703770 / $17.99
VOL. 157 – FLEETWOOD MAC	00101382 / $16.99
VOL. 158 – ULTIMATE CHRISTMAS	00101889 / $14.99
VOL. 159 – WES MONTGOMERY	00102593 / $19.99
VOL. 160 – T-BONE WALKER	00102641 / $16.99
VOL. 161 – THE EAGLES – ACOUSTIC	00102659 / $17.99
VOL. 162 – THE EAGLES HITS	00102667 / $17.99
VOL. 163 – PANTERA	00103036 / $17.99
VOL. 164 – VAN HALEN 1986-1995	00110270 / $17.99
VOL. 166 – MODERN BLUES	00700764 / $16.99
VOL. 168 – KISS	00113421 / $16.99
VOL. 169 – TAYLOR SWIFT	00115982 / $16.99
VOL. 170 – THREE DAYS GRACE	00117337 / $16.99
VOL. 171 – JAMES BROWN	00117420 / $16.99
VOL. 172 – THE DOOBIE BROTHERS	00119670 / $16.99
VOL. 174 – SCORPIONS	00122119 / $16.99
VOL. 175 – MICHAEL SCHENKER	00122127 / $16.99
VOL. 176 – BLUES BREAKERS WITH JOHN MAYALL & ERIC CLAPTON	00122132 / $19.99
VOL. 177 – ALBERT KING	00123271 / $16.99
VOL. 178 – JASON MRAZ	00124165 / $17.99
VOL. 179 – RAMONES	00127073 / $16.99
VOL. 180 – BRUNO MARS	00129706 / $16.99
VOL. 181 – JACK JOHNSON	00129854 / $16.99
VOL. 182 – SOUNDGARDEN	00138161 / $17.99
VOL. 184 – KENNY WAYNE SHEPHERD	00138258 / $17.99
VOL. 187 – JOHN DENVER	00140839 / $17.99

Complete song lists available online.

Prices, contents, and availability subject to change without notice.

HAL•LEONARD® CORPORATION
7777 W. BLUEMOUND RD. P.O. BOX 13819 MILWAUKEE, WI 53213
www.halleonard.com